Sweat, Scale, $ell

Sweat, Scale, $ell

Build Your Business into an Asset of Value™

Pavlo Phitidis

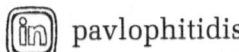 pavlophitidis

 pavlobiz

 pavlophitidis

MACMILLAN

Note from the author

I have recreated events and conversations from my memories of them. In order to maintain their anonymity in some instances, I have changed the names of individuals, as well as some identifying characteristics and details.

First published in 2019
by Pan Macmillan South Africa
Private Bag X19,
Northlands
Johannesburg
2116

www.panmacmillan.co.za

ISBN 978-1-77010-673-4
eISBN 978-1-77010-674-1

© Pavlo Phitidis 2019

All rights reserved. No part of this publication may be reproduced, stored in a retrieval system, or transmitted in any form or by any means, electronic, mechanical, photocopying, recording, or otherwise, without the prior permission of both the copyright owners and the publisher of this edition of the book.

Editing by Wesley Thompson
Proofreading by Sean Fraser
Design and typesetting by Triple M Design
Cover design by publicide

Printed and bound by

*To my business partner and co-creator at Aurik,
Carien Engelbrecht, who took a chance on a dream,
and with her capable hands and always-on brain,
helped shape it and build it into something that
will change the world.*

*To the many business owners we've worked with,
whose troubles and successes, trust and belief,
co-created what we have today to the advantage of
the many others we will work with in future.*

*To the growing team of Aurikites,
boisterous and considered, passionate and pragmatic,
in the past and the future, for breathing life into
what we collectively do.*

*And to Jack, my good friend, whose courage,
creativity and care in building his Asset of Value
significantly shaped and inspired Aurik.*

Contents

Preface ix

Introduction 1

Chapter 1: Failing to Build an Asset of Value 22

Chapter 2: A Business is Like a Ship 39

Chapter 3: Defining an Asset of Value 50

Chapter 4: Building an Asset of Value 56

Chapter 5: Purpose and Positioning 66

Chapter 6: Building a System of Delivery 106

Chapter 7: Your Team 127

Chapter 8: Your Time 147

Chapter 9: Accelerating Growth 156

Chapter 10: Innovation 180

Chapter 11: The Asset of Value Formula 201

Chapter 12: Measuring an Asset of Value 207

Chapter 13: Buffett is Buying 215

Chapter 14: Different Kinds of Business Sales 224

Conclusion: You are in Control 243

Notes 246

Preface

A terrifying reality often discovered too late by business owners is that 94.6% of businesses started never get sold.[1] Yet, there are only two destinations for every business: sale or closure!

Businesses close at tremendous cost to owners and their family, staff, suppliers and customers. This is a woeful end to something that has taken courage to start, creativity to do differently and care to sustain.

Some business owners realise this danger earlier than others, but most don't realise it until it is too late. And time runs out. In fact, it runs away from you in your 40s but sprints from you in your 50s. It is simply not enough to believe that because you have invested all your funds and energy into your business it will deliver an eventual payday. Whereas you need idealism to start and build a business, you need pragmatism to ensure you have built a saleable asset.

Realising that your business might not be a ticket to a safe and comfortable retirement starts with fear but morphs into doubt over time, infecting the essence of who you are, what you will become and how you see the world.

Having witnessed family members fall into this trap, and motivated to help others avoid it, I have spent the last 25 years building businesses. With my business partner Carien Engelbrecht, at Aurik Business Accelerator we have built 12 businesses and helped nearly 2 000 business owners across four continents develop a new perspective on how to build a business that is more asset than emotion, a business that can someday be sold.

There is a remarkable amount of information out there on business strategy. However, most of it is superficial, repeating well-worn, tired advice, making for shallow reading, and propped up with jargon and theoretical swagger but lacking in practical application.

Business owners are practical people. Yet, we are also deeply emotional, and it is our attitudes – how we choose to look at our businesses – that make for success. Why you do what you do as a business owner – monthly, weekly, daily – holds the key to building your business into a saleable asset.

As a business owner, time is your most valuable resource. You want access to a method that works and is presented simply, acting as a guide to help you build your business.

For this reason, I have tried to present our method through stories. Stories work best for us as entrepreneurs. It's through story that we can truly see ourselves. As emotional beings building our dreams, reading the stories of others allows us to reflect, gain insight, practise foresight and, in a non-defensive manner, embrace the most certain path to success.

We start with Aurik's story – how Carien and I found our

Preface

purpose in building businesses and helping owners develop their own enterprises into saleable assets, and in so doing discovered a method, a practical set of activities and steps, and a mindset of building businesses that we call the Asset of Value approach.

The Asset of Value method differs from most others we are taught about how to build a business. An Asset of Value business is a customer-centric enterprise that enjoys consistent revenue, is built on systems that operate smoothly without you, the business owner, being constantly required to get involved, and is supported by a reliable and purposeful team. It is a business that frees your time to focus on growth and innovation. And finally, it is your greatest wealth-generating asset, a business that is ultimately saleable.

We move on to Clive's story, which demonstrates some of the causes and consequences of failing to build an Asset of Value. On the face of it, Clive was a very successful business owner operating in the IT sector. He had a nice home, fully paid off, a holiday home, and had funded his children's education, even managing to send one of his sons to university to study Medicine. But on closer inspection, Clive was a desperate man running full speed down a runway with little tar left and a cliff on the other side.

Then there is Jack, a 54-year-old baker who wanted to sell his business that he began when he was 29 years old. Through Jack's story, we see how building a business into an Asset of Value is not easy and takes time. His journey with me evinces the actions, logic, and mindset needed to build an Asset of

Value. Jack's turnover grew from an eight- to a ten-figure number in nine years.

Ismail works with us through a process of understanding how to rebuild his luxury-product retail business into a problem-solving investment business that grows his revenue annually despite a global recession and a persistent low-growth environment in South Africa.

Themba and I follow a similar journey. The story of how he turned his pump business into a digital one, focused on solving problems for customers rather than simply offering them a service, demonstrates how to build a modern business that can scale even in a depressed economy and a sector fraught with price competition. Themba's business developed a distinct advantage, separating him from his competitors, and would eventually fetch a much higher price.

James and Annie, whose business supplied jewellery display products and which competed with businesses that relied on Chinese imports, reshaped and grew their business by solving their customers' growth problem.

We live through Oren's pain, frustration and rage of trying to find the right skills and talent to support the growth of his data-services business.

There is also Patrick, in the construction industry, who found a way to give his business a distinct advantage by narrowing his focus, but who chose to fail by chasing revenue and not learning to say no to all who walked through his doors.

Through all these stories, we tackle the following challenges, among others:

Preface

- How to create a unique business identity that your customers value and that distinguishes you from your competitors in a noisy market;
- How to create a strategy that remains relevant and resilient in a constantly changing socio-political and economic environment;
- How to create a systems-driven business that generates consistent leads and customers and, through that, steady revenue;
- How to eliminate operational chaos and ensure the simple, scalable and reliable delivery of your services and products;
- How to get the right people to do the right thing at the right time, including bringing your business strategy into the hands, minds and hearts of your employees;
- How to manufacture time for yourself through the design of your business;
- How to invest your time in developing smart strategies and performing activities that accelerate the growth and value of your business;
- How to craft innovation into your business's design so that it deepens value for your customers, reduces your chaos and costs and creates revenue to support your business valuation; and
- How businesses are valued, bought and sold.

Through these stories of ordinary business owners, people like you and me, we will see what actions to take and what mindset to adopt in order to build successful businesses. The lessons that emerge through these stories are accessible and relevant to every business owner, irrespective of the size of your business and the sector you operate in, and you can learn from and apply them in your business immediately. The Asset of Value method breaks building a business down to its simplest truth, and in that it becomes a reference guide for your next steps in your own business-building journey.

As business owners, we risk everything we have to build our businesses. We do so with little support from government. And yet we create jobs and contribute enormously to tax revenue. But instead of allowing blame to infect our attitude, we must focus on what we have control over: our attitudes and the actions we take to develop sound businesses that one day will fetch the price we deserve as a reward for the years of sacrifice and risk.

I hope that this book will guide you to adopt a new mindset and that you will apply the Asset of Value method on your journey to creating your greatest wealth-generating asset.

Introduction

'I can't change the direction of the wind, but I can adjust my sails to always reach my destination.' – Jimmy Dean

A few days after we launched Aurik Business Incubator, Carien and I received a phone call from a business owner who had found us via our website. Our site was one we had put together in the days when Google was easier to understand and good content alone, rather than ad spend, gave you a better search ranking. It was a good website, I thought.

Our 'office' was, in effect, a stationery cupboard in an architect's office. The architect also allowed us to use the boardroom when clients visited. Our first piece of furniture was a rather long table that stretched out the room, aggravating all who passed up and down the busy corridor. Carien sat opposite me. A more different person to me could not be found.

The phone rang. We were full of anticipation.

'Aurik Business Incubator, how can we help you?' Carien answered in a calm tone.

Listening in on speaker-phone, I heard a gruff male voice on

Sweat, Scale, $ell

the other end of the line: 'I need incubation help.'

'One minute, sir,' Carien said, 'I'll put you through to the right division.'

That was me, across the table. An entire division. We both looked at the other phone, on my side of the table. How many times should it ring for us to sound big? Not corporate, but more than two rings. At least more than zero customers to date, a few days after opening. Carien put him through.

I couldn't resist it: on the third ring, I picked up the receiver, put the call on speaker, and answered, 'Aurik Business Incubator, how can I help you?'

What a painful experience it was to have to take this call with Carien, an obsessive-compulsive, controlling perfectionist, listening in. Carien's qualities are fine ones to have if you are building a business that lives or dies on delivery, quality and impact, but I needed to do this deal, whatever it was and whatever it meant. We had launched, the clock was ticking towards bankruptcy and time to revenue was vital. We needed to pay for the stationery cupboard and have some money left over to put food on the table.

'So, you do incubation?' the man growled.

'Yes, we do, sir. How can I assist?'

A brief silence followed as he took his breath. I could hear he was a big man.

'Do you work in White River?'

Now, of course we didn't. It was 350 kilometres away. In those days we were a proximity-based business.

'Yes sir,' I answered, and determinedly looking Carien directly in the eye, and added, 'how can we help you?'

Carien glared at me. She raised her finger, shaking it vigorously, indicating, 'NO.'

'I'm looking for incubation support to hatch 7 000 chicken eggs a week to sell the chicks to neighbouring farmers.'

The pause that followed felt like a lifetime of silence. I felt like a deer in the headlights. What did he just ask for? Was this real? Who was this man? Was it a friend teasing us shortly after our launch, playing a cruel joke? Why would the man have asked us for help incubating chicken eggs when our website clearly stated that we offered *business* incubation? I felt my fury rise and quelled it immediately. I took a deep breath, paused, exhaled and calmly asked, 'When would you need delivery, sir?'

He set a deadline. I replied, 'No problem, sir,' and Carien and I got to work after a vicious fight about our raison d'être. The internet is wonderful.

We found blueprints for chicken-egg incubators and searched for videos to help guide us. Another of Carien's strong points is her remarkable intellect and studious nature. We learned about chicken diseases and ways to keep chickens healthy and happy. We designed the incubators so enthusiastically that I thought this was actually the business we would go into. We visited a friend who could help us with the construction of the incubators. A week later, our quote accepted, a deposit paid, manufacture began. Four weeks later, on low-bed trailers, six egg-to-chick incubators were shipped to a farm 350 kilometres away. Our bank account brimmed with full payment.

With rent settled for the next six months and some money left over for food and coffee, we realised we had a problem. What happens when you build a business that you know will offer value but that your market doesn't even know it needs? What do you do when your concept is so new that your potential clients have never even heard of it before? We thought that including the word 'incubator' in our name would allow people to know what we were all about, but the market associated us with something else. Chickens. While the poultry industry is a big and important one in South Africa, our mission and vision was not to feed a nation.

Our vision was to make the world a better place by helping people who have the courage, creativity and care to start and sustain a business to grow their concerns and inspire others to emulate their success. But here was the problem: even with all their courage, creativity and care, most business owners are not successful. Most new businesses fail, and many that operate successfully for decades are closed or get lamely handed over to family or management. The handover is often portrayed to unsuspecting family or management as an opportunity but is largely a way for the entrepreneur to secure an earning to live off.

Are entrepreneurs born or made?
My dad, uncles and others in my family were all entrepreneurs. They had what it took to succeed. They were educated and smart, stuck it out in their industries and came from entrepreneurial families with some access to capital. But all

Introduction

of them failed to grow Assets of Value businesses. If even *they* had failed, with all these fine advantages and qualities, after decades of being in business, what more was needed to succeed?

My earliest childhood memories are of my father sitting at the table on Sunday mornings surrounded by piles of papers and files, an electronic, plug-in calculator, pencils, punches, staplers and notepads. Sunday mornings were all about costings, debtors and creditors. He seconded me into the activity.

My dad's business was an importer and distributor of outdoor and leisure merchandise such as camping equipment, pocketknives, fishing lures and sports goods. My job was to prepare the brochures for the sales representatives. This entailed cutting out black-and-white, photocopied pictures of the products, placing them on an A4 sheet of white paper, presenting the layout to my dad, who would make a few adjustments, and then gluing them on the sheet until the page was done.

My dad would make about a hundred copies and the brochures were ready for the sales representatives for the week. I excelled in hand-eye coordination and learned numeracy and literacy fast at school due to those Sunday exercises from the age of four.

Later in life, I would be distressed to see people I loved, respected and admired fail to build their businesses into concerns that could leave a legacy, help the next generation get a better start in life and be sold for a capital gain. I was even more distressed that failed entrepreneurship seemed to be genetic.

It was only later, after spending some time in Palo Alto, the epicentre of Silicone Valley, that I gained new insight. There I saw the vibrancy of one of the most exciting, entrepreneurial locations at work. The best and the brightest people from all over the world flocked to Palo Alto. Investors hung in the skies like vultures looking for the next great brain, idea or emerging business. Venture capitalists and other funders swam in the turbulent waters like crocodiles looking for their next meal of talent. Even governments from around the world, and universities, hankered after opportunities. Here I learned from data available from the Internal Revenue Service (IRS) that 94.6% of all businesses started fail to sell – this in arguably what was then the world's most vibrant and enabling business environment, with business-friendly policies, in a nation that admires, respects and celebrates entrepreneurs.

I was glad to know that entrepreneurial failure was not in my DNA. This was a global phenomenon. But more importantly, I had found a problem worth solving! The seed of Aurik was planted.

A vision is born

Our vision was to change this broken system. We single-mindedly wanted to serve people who relentlessly endured the many challenges it takes to build a business. We wanted to dramatically flip the odds of exit success in their favour. We would commit our life purpose to this, and it would become the future source of all our meaning.

Hence chickens! Can you imagine that? A bold idea, a life

purpose, and an idealistic passion translated into a call that led to chicken incubators. I realised we had a problem and that's when our journey truly began.

As any good entrepreneurs attempting to launch something novel would do, we became our own customers first by building businesses of our own and learning from our successes and failures. Idealism and concepts alone wouldn't cut it – we needed to figure out, through practical steps and action, what we offered, who we offered it to, and how we would deliver our service.

Every business owner should have a bold vision, something much bigger than one's own personal experience and worldview. It should be daunting and intimidating at first. This is important because a bold vision, something that is both exciting and frightening at the same time, feeds your passion and energy. If your vision is about making the world a better place by creating better options for the people who you want to serve through your business, that idea in itself, about creating a better world or experience, can and hopefully will, over time, become an obsession. That idea needs to root itself deeply in your person and being. It will then fuel your resilience, drive and energy in building a business in a competitive, overcrowded world.

Just as a tree finds its energy from the youngest leaf – the leaf at the very top of the tree, the one that holds the promise of what the tree can become, and the one that stretches into the endless, empty space where the sun's rays can be absorbed – your vision should reach into the future and draw on the energy and resilience that the journey of building a business demands. The acronym SME means Small to Medium Enterprise. It is used as a descriptor of businesses that typically generate annual revenues between say, R1m to R200m. Depending on who is using the acronym, the sizes of the business included vary. Corporates, governments, educational institutions and other stakeholders in our economy use the word to define us, the private business owner. Their use of the acronym sees us all being treated as one amorphous, unruly mass. When we speak about political parties or corporates, we give them a uniqueness, a distinction. Yet, we are the engines of the economy. It is the private business owner that is the most vested player in any economy globally. We invest our own money and make direct sacrifices to build and grow businesses against formidable odds all to be amassed into a diminishing term, SME. I am yet to meet a small business owner. I only meet a growing business owner. The alternative acronym, SMB, meaning Small to Medium Business, is what I use. It feels like it holds more dignity and offers so much more potential to society and its owner.

It would be naive to romanticise big ideas without recognising that the bigger they are, the bigger their shadow. We wanted to place SMBs at the centre of government policy, economic thinking and societal admiration so that SMBs could get the just attention they deserve, but our journey attracted hordes of naysayers, generated profound levels of frustration and created a resistance to change from business owners themselves, corporates who wanted to retain the status quo, and even governments. You will undoubtedly face similar resistance, but having a bold, mostly clear vision will ensure that you stay the course.

A product is built

We benefited from a well-articulated and consistent vision. Nearly a decade after launching Aurik, our results are remarkable. In 2018, while the South African economy grew by a meagre 0.8%, our portfolio of 302 business-owner clients grew their revenue by 29.8% on average. In all of them, I saw my father and his brothers. In all of them, I saw Carien and myself. But how did we ensure that we manifested our bold vision? Our idealism in wanting to serve entrepreneurs was not enough if we could not build a business that could consistently deliver on its promises. Idealism can have a dark side to it. If it is not actualised in practical terms, it can consume you. We've met many entrepreneurs who, driven by idealism, over the years have become angry and resentful about how 'unfair' the world is as they have found their vision reduced to a daily slog for survival.

Did we seriously think, after our initial success of supplying the chicken-egg incubators, of going into the business? Our success surely meant that there was a gap! But we weren't turned on by chicken-egg incubators. Affinity is important, and that is something that so-called 'serial entrepreneurs' don't get. To simply go in the direction of money, where the deals lie and a quick buck can be made, does not build a business that, in my experience, you will be able to provide with the unforgiving levels of focus, attention and energy required to stay ahead of your competitors.

We needed to find a way to enable our idealism through action. And so a nine-year journey began of starting, building and selling 12 businesses across different sectors and industries. We built these businesses with knowledgeable and capable partners, and we built them fast. Although there were many dark hours, days and weeks, in retrospect it was an intense, all-consuming and fun time.

It was a journey that would see us deliver two failures, two listings on the Johannesburg Stock Exchange (JSE), conclude three sales through Management Buy-Outs (MBOs) and five sales to corporate buyers. We secured nearly 11 times our money back, which we later learned was considered a brilliant return.

Most valuably, these years gave us the pragmatic foundation of what Aurik needed to do to realise its idealistic vision. The last handful of businesses took only 50% of the time and 35% of the capital investment to build to the same value as the first handful of businesses.

We realised that we had discovered something remarkable, something that could change the world! If only we could consolidate what we had learned into a method and a plan of action, we could help business owners get the same results using our approach.

Our results were not sector-driven, because we had built our businesses across many different sectors. They were not owing to our gifted business partners, because we consistently achieved the results across a portfolio. Our success was due to our method of building businesses. At first, we were not aware of what it was that had enabled this, so we began analysing our successes and failures.

We considered our failures first. Why had two of our businesses failed? Why had some of our businesses nearly failed? We looked at the fights we'd had with customers, staff, suppliers and partners across all the businesses. Why had they happened and how did they end? What could we have done to avoid them? Where should we have invested more money into the businesses and why hadn't we realised that we needed to do so? What would we have gained from avoiding the fights? We analysed the performance of each business over time against each other. We drew from industry and sector statistics and visited staff who were still employed in the businesses that we sold. We also visited the customers and suppliers we had worked with. In each business, we looked both internally and externally, and the questions were endless.

Finding a business partner
Mostly, Carien and I debated, argued, fought and almost killed each other. Building 12 businesses in nine years created remarkable stress and pressure.

How we met and became business partners was more a coincidence than a well-devised strategy. I had just come back from the USA, and with Aurik in mind, I had to earn some money. I took up a three-year stint at the University of the Witwatersrand Business School as an external examiner of Master of Business Administration (MBA) papers on company valuations.

Sweat, Scale, $ell

The MBA students, as part of their corporate-finance elective, had to select a company listed on the JSE and value it using three techniques, and I had been given a pile of their papers to mark. I skimmed through the first handful of papers to get a sense of the standard of work and then proceeded to attempt to read the handwriting and figure out the calculations and arguments of the students. A week later, I received a phone call.

'Are you Pavlo?' the person asked.

'Yes, who is this and how can I help?' I responded equally abruptly.

'I'm Carien. My lecturer said I need to come and see you about my valuation paper that you apparently marked.'

Carien went on to explain that she was not happy with the mark of a C I had given her and wanted to 'better understand the reasoning for it'.

We met a week later and reviewed the paper. Carien had only used one valuation technique when the question required three. The one she used was very well applied, accurate, intelligent and of a very high standard. The fact that Carien only answered one-third of the question was the reason that she won a C and nothing more. Carien was incensed until she realised this. She went on to say that I was the first-ever examiner, post-schooling, post her legal degree, post her master's degree, who had ever given her anything less than a distinction.

Was this a fellow obsessive-compulsive perfection-disorder comrade? This and her previous work history on large-scale development and project management made her the perfect business partner to manifest Aurik's vision. At the time, Aurik was only an idea, and Carien had a slew of employment offers from established companies.

I had to make Aurik sound bigger than it was at that time to convince Carien to work with me, so I said, 'Join me now and I'll put up a bank guarantee for your first year's salary.'

We made a deal, leaving me to figure out how to put up a bank guarantee – something I'm yet to do today!

Learning through doing
You cannot be an expert on all the elements required to make a business successful. If you want to grow your business, you need partners and a team with the requisite skills and knowledge that you don't possess yourself.

Today, Carien and I still fight, debate and argue passionately, and we exhaust our team and ourselves over details that can incrementally improve the quality of the client's experience and impact on their business performance. But what held us together as business partners was the vision of what we wanted to build, and the fact that we were on the verge of inventing something remarkable. It wasn't all a fight. Often, frustrated at not finding clarity in what we were building, we would stop debating and direct our focus on analysing the businesses some of our first clients were building.

It dawned on me that I was developing the skill of listening, of asking questions rather than giving answers, and interpreting what was being said rather than how it was being said. This skill remains key to our success. It's all about being hard on the issues but soft on the person. I honed this ability over time, practised it with every engagement and found it to be very powerful.

Clients often ask me: 'How do you know if something will work in business?' This is a question about experience that plagues most business owners. During those early years, Carien and I often had cause to worry whether things would work. We discovered that the answer to this question is found in action alone. Building a business is artisanal; it's not an academic whiteboard exercise. It grows through many steps, interactions and actions that help you see what works and what doesn't.

Malcolm Gladwell argues in his book *Outliers: The Story of Success* that it takes 10 000 hours to become an expert at something. While I agree, I believe it takes 10 000 mistakes in doing something before you can become an expert at it. Carien and I certainly earned our 10 000 hours. But more than that, we made 10 000 mistakes. We learned a great deal from those errors.

Success in business does not come from reading a book, watching a movie or browsing the internet for business advice. The effort it took us to build our businesses, the school fees we paid, the 14-hour days we worked, and the youth we sacrificed helped shine a light clearly and brightly on what worked, what didn't, and how to build a business in the shortest time and the cheapest way possible.

You can be whatever you want but you can't be everything
We now had to figure out how to articulate our vision to the

most important audience: our customers. Who were they, what mattered to them and how would we create a language and a tone that would resonate deeply with them? During this time, our debates intensified.

We argued over the name 'Aurik Business Incubator'. We fought over who our customers were. I was nervous about limiting our scope whereas Carien wanted a tighter definition of customer. I was driven by a fear of cashflow problems while Carien was concerned about impact and quality.

In the beginning, we were all things to all people. We worked with any business owner: you could be starting up, established, facing bankruptcy, wanting to buy a business or sell one, dealing with family, staff, debtor or creditor issues; we would help you. This helped our cashflow, but it created chaos in our operations and ability to deliver. We learned many valuable, difficult and important lessons.

Eventually, we gained clarity in terms of who we should be serving. This required constantly re-evaluating and adapting our focus. We would try to articulate what we stood for and what we did, and then we would hold this position until it was invalidated by newfound insight and knowledge. Each time, we would change the website, the language we used and the logo. It cost money and time. Getting it right was critical and I was obsessed. Carien was irritated.

We agreed not to service distressed businesses to narrow down and better understand our customers. We then agreed not to serve start-up business owners. This was tough for me. It was where I had come from. These are the people who have the courage to start a business, mostly undercapitalised and under stressful conditions, and to dig deeply into their creativity, daring to do things differently, and facing endless rejection from those who don't share their vision. This takes tremendous fortitude. Each rejection feels like a rejection of yourself. This is no different to an artist facing a negative critique on a piece of work that he or she believes to be his or her greatest creative expression. Surely, I thought, these are the qualities – which justified the greatest rewards – that we should be in service of at Aurik?

We then decided to narrow our focus further and only serve established businesses with annual revenue between $1m and $30m. The businesses Carien and I had built and sold were all in this band. It was clear that we understood the challenges and mindset of business owners traversing this stage of the business lifecycle best. It was also evident from our activities that this was where we had the greatest impact and could deliver a consistent, quality experience. Carien was thrilled. I was warming up to the idea. I understood that if we served any customers outside of our agreed revenue band, this would cause operational chaos and hell between Carien and me. I now knew what Leonardo da Vinci meant when he said, 'Simplicity is the ultimate sophistication.'

Now we needed to change our name. We agreed on 'Aurik Business Accelerator'. That was easy given that we had a clear focus on serving established businesses. Finally, we had to define what we did for our customers. We needed a simple phrase that would capture intuitively in the minds of our customers what they could expect from us.

After what felt like hundreds of debates and arguments, we reached a consensus. Getting ideas that are well formed in your head into clear language that resonates emotively with your customers is arguably the hardest challenge that an ambitious business faces.

There are a number of techniques you can use to get this right. We kept it simple. I visited 32 current and former clients over a week. After many meetings, we began to identify the problems that we solved for our customers and why it mattered to them. These were things that we already knew. We had experienced them ourselves but we had complicated matters to such a degree that we were trapped in our own world, our own thought processes. It was noisy, and yet, with all our intelligence, work and commitment, we could not distil the simple words needed to explain what we did. So, we left it. We reshaped the website with the new name and got on with doing our business.

Creating a unique identity

Gold began a bull run in 2005, its price increasing from $500 to $800 per ounce over the period of a year.

South Africa is obsessed with gold. We have some of the deepest mines in the world, and our gold-mining industry provides vital jobs and forms the basis for a broad industrial base. However, the mining sector has been in decline since 2006.

We had a number of clients working in and around the gold-mining industry. One of these was Themba, a pump technician who was in the business of supplying pumps to the mines to remove waste water from mine shafts. Themba was therefore directly investing in an already overcrowded and highly competitive space.

I argued vigorously with Themba, warning him that the sector was in decline and that the mines were placing vicious pressure on suppliers to regulate and drop their prices.

'But, Pavlo, you don't understand,' Themba pleaded. 'Gold is a real asset. Our country was built on the back of it. In fact, I am already up on the shares I bought!'

I immediately countered: 'Themba, this was not the deal between us. The deal was that your business is going to be built into your greatest wealth-generating asset. When we met, you were chasing deals, going from one to another in a never-ending cycle. That'll never build your business into something that can be sold at the end of the day. An asset is something that accumulates value for you as an investor in three ways. Think of it as a share on the stock exchange. Firstly, you get your value as an investor from the free cash that the company you invested in generates from its trading activities. These are called dividends. Secondly, by taking some of that cash and reinvesting it into growth and new opportunities, you increase the share's equity value or capital value. So, if you buy a share at R50, you'd hope to sell it in the future for more than R50. That's a capital gain. And thirdly, it's tradable. You can sell that share. Your business should be built to deliver that outcome. It should be built into an asset!'

The penny dropped. There it was. *That's what we do at*

Aurik. We work with business owners to build their businesses into assets. It was crisp, simple, clear and it said it all.

I raced back to Aurik. I burst into Carien's office. 'It's all about Assets of Value,' I explained. 'We work with established business owners to build their businesses into Assets of Value!'

She got up from her chair and walked to the whiteboard. In her nearly illegible handwriting, she scribbled 'Asset of Value' and stepped back.

I was like a puppy that had just dug up a dirty old bone and brought it enthusiastically into the house to show my owner. All I needed now was a pat on the head and to be told, 'Good boy!'

Carien then wrote 'established business owners' and paused. Turning to me, she said, 'We will measure our performance using two metrics: quality and impact.' She wrote them on the board. We would measure quality by our customers' experience of working with us, and our impact would be determined by the performance of their businesses.

I loved it. Carien loved it. It was complex yet so simple. The ceaseless debates and arguments that tested the fabric of our partnership; the abyss of self-doubt that we had endured; and the challenge to find the simple words to express our vision – these were all worth it. Ideas are only actionable once captured in simple words.

With clarity on what we did and who we did it for, we drew confidence that we could deliver results. Our approach was original, steeped in practice rather than theory, and we got ready to accelerate Aurik.

- ❏ Most businesses started never get sold. Instead, they are closed at great cost to the business owner and her or his family. This is because most businesses are not built for sale from the start. Instead, they are built for a lifestyle.
- ❏ Create a bold vision that is bigger than you, your business and what you believe is immediately possible. A big vision, along with affinity for what you do, will make you resilient. Then find a way to act on that vision by capturing what you do in simple words.
- ❏ When you start out, take on any business that comes your way, even if this means designing and building chicken-egg incubators. This will generate cashflow and funding, even if the work is not aligned to your vision.
- ❏ Find a business partner who will help you build faster and work smarter and more confidently. A good business partner should not have the same skill set as you but should share your values and goals. Develop tolerance and patience to listen to your partner and learn from what he or she has to offer.
- ❏ Reflect constantly on what does and doesn't work. It is necessary to make many mistakes in order to become an expert in what you do. Learning from them will give you the insights, foresight and wisdom to thrive in your industry and sector. Identify better ways to do things and take responsibility for everything in the business, especially the things that go wrong.
- ❏ Narrow the focus of your business by listening to what your customers want and need. Once you have done this, don't

try to be all things to all people, since you'll end up becoming nothing to everyone. We live and work in a world that is becoming smaller and more competitive than ever before. Choose to build a business that becomes expert in a field and narrow your focus to deepen that expertise.

❑ The job of every business owner should be to build their business into an **Asset of Value**. We, at Aurik, discovered a method to building such a business, and we share this approach with you in this book.

❑ This book will help you build your business into your greatest wealth-generating asset – one that will reward you for your endless effort, creativity and care.

Chapter 1

Failing to Build an Asset of Value

'The only real mistake is the one from which we learn nothing.'
– Henry Ford

Early on in Aurik's existence, I met Clive, a business owner in the IT sector who was having trouble getting the right terms for the sale of his business. Clive had heard of us from a friend of a friend and wanted to see if we could help.

Comfort is the cancer of your potential
Clive was the most unassuming entrepreneur. As a kid, he was seldom invited to other children's birthday parties. He told me it wasn't malicious. Mostly, he said, the kids just forgot to put him on the list.

'That's how unremarkable I was back then,' he joked.

He finished school. Only just. 'I hated it,' he told me, and then as quickly corrected himself: 'Hate would suggest I cared about it or something.'

His parents worried that he would amount to nothing and they would have to continue supporting him.

Failing to Build an Asset of Value

'I would have felt the same way if I were in their position,' he mused.

As time went by, Clive spent his days watching mindless TV. He put on weight. While he had gone for a few job interviews, his lack of skills and poor results in personality assessments caused him to fail. Time passed and Clive faded even further into insignificance.

'Can you believe that that's what I thought everyone's life was like?' he ruminated.

One evening, his father, coming home from work, brought a newspaper and gave it to Clive. He insisted Clive consider three of the advertised jobs he had found in the classifieds.

Listlessly, Clive took the paper and, in the days to come, sent in his application for one of the jobs. On the day of the interview, he dutifully reported for breakfast before he left with his father for the city. That afternoon, Clive's parents waited eagerly for him to return. He got back home by bus and walked through the door.

'How did it go?' probed his mother.

'Fine,' Clive said, opening the fridge and looking for something to eat.

'Did you like any of the opportunities?' his father pressed.

'Yip, they were okay,' said Clive.

His parents felt deflated. They had tried many times in the last two years to get his life off to a start.

Later, the phone rang. Clive's mother answered it and called him from the TV. 'It's for you,' she shouted and went back to the ironing.

That evening, as the family ate pudding and when Clive's sister had finished telling everyone about her day, Clive said: 'I have some news, too.'

Startled, they all looked up.

'You have news? What news?' asked his father.

'I got a job with a company called IBM,' Clive mumbled.

The job was really an apprenticeship. There were seven slots available and nine people applied. Nobody quite understood what the job was about. Of the nine applicants, only seven arrived and the company had to fill the slots.

When you find your gift, never give up on it

Clive metamorphosed. He came to life in his apprenticeship. He was a connectivity technician and his job was to make machines 'see and talk' to each other. His parents neither knew nor cared what it all meant. They were simply relieved to get him out of the house. Clive discovered that he had a natural affinity for the work. He could speak 'geek'. He excelled in the job and spent most of his time at the company. One day, the employees of IBM were called together and told that IBM had decided to withdraw from South Africa for political reasons. Clive slumped.

'It's the only thing that I had ever done that had meant anything to me,' he said.

But if you have the right attitude, change can present opportunity. Clive and a few former IBM employees were offered the chance to set up a company to take over servicing a few of IBM's former clients.

'Running a business was harder than doing the actual work,'

Failing to Build an Asset of Value

Clive told me. 'At the same time, I was getting married. You should have seen the faces of the people I told who knew me,' he said with a wry smile. 'They could not hide their astonishment. Me, Clive, someone wanted to marry *me*! To this day I remain astonished!' he laughed.

Clive lived and loved what he did. It helped that the world of IT was coming alive. He was in a growth market, and naturally his business grew, from a one-man show to two people, three, and then five.

'Employing people – well, I thought it would be fun. It wasn't. Finding the right people is hard, especially when you are so busy. You have no time to consider if a person is right or not and you are desperate for help. I hated it and I'm not a people's person at all.'

I was gripped by Clive's story. He had a dry sense of self-deprecating humour, something he had cultivated to cope with life. I also had respect for Clive, a man who seemingly had nothing going for him, finding his passion more by mistake than deliberate action, and starting and running a business that by the time we met employed 89 people, making him one of the most established medium-sized IT network businesses in the sector.

Clive was in his 60s when I first met him. He had been building his business over the last 25 years. He was the epitome of success for his friends, family and colleagues. He had a very nice home, fully paid off. He had a holiday home, too, at the coast, almost paid off. Almost all of his kids were finished school, and one had gone to university to study Medicine.

Over the previous eight years, Clive and his family had taken overseas holidays every second year. He wanted his kids to see the world, something he was not afforded in his childhood. His daughter was interested in horse riding, and he indulged her in it, proud of her accomplishments. He was a great dad. His wife Debbie forgave his absences because she knew he was building the family business for her and the kids.

Clive's business buzzed. He was always busy. He loved what he did and was good at it. His favourite work was to find the ghosts in the machines, solving connectivity and performance problems in customers' technology infrastructure. He had also built his business with some good relationships and great deals. Clive had secured the exclusive distribution rights on various hardware items such as routers, printers and boosters. These were good agencies and the envy of his competitors. An IT network business with 68 staff is a busy business.

Clive felt it. In fact, a few years back, he hadn't been feeling well. Concerned, Debbie had told him to go for a check-up. He had been tossing and turning at night and she knew that it had to be the business or something at work that led to his restlessness. He lied and told her that he had been to see the doctor and that everything was fine.

'At that point,' Clive defended, 'I had no time. With 68 staff all needing me and customers wanting me, it was becoming impossible. My passion for the business was waning and it felt like a daily slog. I was central to almost everything.'

Failing to Build an Asset of Value

A few months later, Clive managed to visit his doctor who promptly sent him for a battery of tests. Clive had had a small heart attack two months back and hadn't even felt it.

'I went home horrified that this had happened, and I told my wife. She was furious. *So much for a woman's empathy*, I thought to myself, but she was right. Her anger was that this had been coming for far too long,' he said glumly.

Clive agreed that Debbie should join him in the business. She had strong administration and people-management skills, the parts of the business Clive liked least. They also agreed to scale the business down. It was an insatiable beast that was growing fast.

'It's just not worth losing you over the business,' Debbie had said.

Clive agreed, though reluctantly – who ever wants to scale down their passion?

The business responded to Debbie's entry. Clive was more focused and less stressed, and he could now focus more on what he was good at doing. Debbie cleaned up the administration of the business. For the first time in the business's history, the back office began to work well. They grew to 89-people strong in the two years since Debbie had joined Clive.

One Monday afternoon after closing time there was a knock at the office door. Clive checked the CCTV and saw a man in a suit waiting outside. Clive went down to see how he could help.

'Clive?' the man asked as Clive opened the door. He held

out his hand, introducing himself as the CEO of a large technology services company listed on the JSE.

Clive shook the man's hand, somewhat surprised and wondering where he had met this man before.

'We haven't met face to face, but I recognise you from LinkedIn,' the man said.

Clive settled him in the meeting room and asked Debbie to join them.

'Clive, you have made my life a misery for a number of years now,' the CEO began, smiling.

Clive and Debbie exchanged a glance, wondering where this was going.

'We have tried to take you out of the market but have failed at every turn. We tried with your international suppliers but they would not give us your agencies. We tried with your customers but they swear by you. We even tried with your key staff but none would leave even though we offered them better salaries.' He paused and waited for Clive to contemplate his message.

Clive looked at him silently, his anger building.

'So, Clive, I am here to say mea culpa – if I can't take you out of the market, maybe, if you are interested, I can take you in.'

'What do you mean, "take me in"?' Clive responded.

'We would like to buy your business, Clive. Lock, stock, and barrel. All in. Is that something you'd be interested in?'

That evening, Clive and Debbie contemplated the proposition. At first, Clive was incensed that the CEO had pitched up at the door and confirmed the suspicions he had about the corporate

Failing to Build an Asset of Value

attacks on his business. He would never sell his business, he thought. At least, he hadn't thought of it in this way. Their son, Kevin, had gone to medical school and their daughter, Jenna, still at school, had absolutely no interest in the business. Clive was approaching 60 and he was feeling the strain in the business.

'It has served us well; *you* have served us well,' Debbie began. 'Our finances are in good stead, the business makes a clean profit and we have very little debt in the family now, Clive.'

It was clear that Debbie wanted to look at the offer more seriously, but Clive needed some time. This was his life. As much as the business had taken its toll on him, it had saved him in many ways. His friends and community came from the business. What would he do afterwards, he wondered? The thought scared him. Since starting this business he had found his value. People needed and wanted him. He remembered the years before, how lost, uninspired, he was.

The second meeting with the CEO a few weeks later was better considered. Clive and Debbie had decided to sell, but at their price. The business was profitable and Clive wanted good money for it. Clive told the CEO they were prepared to sell and stated his price: R42 million. Clive knew the worth of his business and that it had legs – growth was in its future; he and Debbie had debated extensively around this fact.

The CEO could see that Clive would be reluctant to sell his business for anything less than R42m, so he agreed to the purchase at Clive's price. Clive received the documents related to the sale in which the price, clearly stated as R42m, was subject to a due diligence.

Clive's accountant explained to him that a due diligence gave the corporation six weeks to check that what Clive had declared regarding the business – its assets, liabilities, commercial potential and other things – was accurate. 'They will want to look at your customer contracts, agency agreements and key staff contracts. It's an accepted norm in the sale of a business.'

Clive was miffed. This, after the buyer had tried to take him out of the market? Debbie went to work to prepare files and Clive reluctantly made himself available to help her. Clive found that the CEO's team was a nice bunch of people. They were discreet and considerate. Clive softened. He and Debbie spoke about a vacation after the sale and where and how they would invest their money. Clive agreed to spend some of it, even though he was a frugal man. He had some ideas about a camper van, to Debbie's horror.

Are you building your business into an asset or a job?
The weeks passed by. Clive's apprehension was building. After nine weeks of waiting, Clive put a call through to the CEO's office.

'Clive,' the CEO answered, 'this is synchronous. I was about to call you and tell you we are done. When can we meet to iron out the finer details?'

They agreed to meet that Friday at Clive's offices. Debbie

Failing to Build an Asset of Value

went first thing in the morning to buy freshly baked croissants and good filter coffee. She was in a celebratory mood.

At 10am sharp, the CEO and his team arrived at the offices.

'Clive, thank you for your patience and tolerance,' the CEO began. 'Due diligence processes are complicated for us. We have to report to the advisors on the JSE and we are legally obliged to make announcements and adhere to a host of regulations. I hated it as much as you probably did, so please accept my apologies for the delay.'

Nice guy, Clive thought. *He seems able to understand things from my point of view, and I feel sorry for him for the red tape he has to get through to get this deal done.*

'So, it's a big day for us all. Debbie, thank you for the delicious croissants and coffee,' the CEO continued, sliding sets of documents across the table to both Clive and Debbie. 'Should we proceed?'

Clive nodded.

'First off, let's get price out the way. Turn to page four.'

Clive anxiously flipped to the page. There it was: R42m as agreed, with the CEO's countersignature next to it as if to emphasise the point. Clive sighed with relief.

'Next, let's look at the payment terms. Turn to page five.'

And there it was: 10% of the price in cash up front, the remaining 90% split over three years against achievement of minimum profits. Furthermore, the payments over three years would be split 30% in cash and 70% paid in shares in the company.

It also stated that Clive would only be able to sell his shares in six months' time.

'It doesn't look good when the seller gets rid of her or his shares in the company,' the CEO explained. 'The market sees this as a sign of the seller lacking confidence in the company and its future!'

Clive would also have to work in the business for three years. Added to that, he would have to commute to the head office, a two-hour drive in peak traffic, whereas previously it had taken him 10 minutes to get to and from work. He would report to a senior manager half his age, a corporate type who knew nothing about IT networks. Finally, he would have no control over finances, reporting, bookkeeping, accounting and human resources. The terms and conditions were onerous.

Clive's heart sank. He had exposed all of the details of his business to this corporate competitor believing that the deal would go smoothly. He quelled his growing fury and feelings of vulnerability and responded coldly, 'We will need to think about the terms. I was not expecting these conditions.'

The CEO replied: 'I can see you are worried about the terms, Clive, but let me tell you why they are necessary …' The CEO went on to provide reasons for the requirements.

Clive and Debbie did not proceed with the sale. A few weeks on, at a social event, a friend recommended that Clive come see me. And here we were.

Clive and Debbie briefed me on their predicament. They left me with the due diligence report, which I studied with interest, and we met again the next day.

Failing to Build an Asset of Value

'Clive and Debbie, I will always back the business owner in any way possible, especially in a sale to a corporate buyer,' I began. 'As the business owner, you have risked everything to build what you have, and you depend on the sale for your pension or financial legacy as a reward for your efforts. You deserve our backing. You have my respect for what you have achieved to date, and I empathise with your frustrations.'

Clive leaned back, and Debbie put her hand on his arm.

'But here's the thing,' I continued. 'This report is very considered. It's fair and accurate in my assessment. I hate to say this, but I agree with the CEO's terms, given his position as head of a company listed on the JSE and the nature of his business. He is not trying to screw you over. I think he genuinely wanted to get this deal done.'

They were both very upset. We agreed to do a diagnostic on the business. This is a process that we at Aurik conduct on all the businesses we work with. It looks at 207 business activities to identify the gaps in the underlying business systems responsible for making the business work. It has a very sobering effect, shining a light on weak spots without making anyone defensive. The outcome corroborated the CEO's due diligence. Clive *was* the business. The business was not built into an Asset of Value. When you are the business, the only way to buy such a business is to buy you. When your business cannot function without you, you don't have a business, you have a job. How do you sell a job?

The best time to plant a tree was 20 years ago, but the second-best time is now

Clive, now in his late 60s, still runs his business. He is in a no-man's land. His business is unaffordable to the average, private buyer. A sale at what Clive would consider a fair price would leave him at the buyer's mercy. What if he and the buyer cannot get on with each other? The buyer would control everything, leaving Clive with few options.

Clive had heard stories of similar deals in which the corporate buyer made it impossible for the business to hit the profit targets to reduce the purchase price or secure the early exit of the seller with the same impact.

The lessons from this very painful experience were simple. Most of us only build one business in our lives. We don't build it in such a way that we know it can one day be sold at a price and for terms and conditions we consider fair. Instead, we build it around our products and people. We build it around ourselves.

Lessons or insights are only beneficial if you act on them to correct the mistakes you have made. If you don't act on your insights, decades later the initial joy you had in starting and running your business will be replaced with regret.

We should rather focus on building our businesses into Assets of Value. If we do so, our passion will not be limited to the products or services we offer but will result from building a systems-driven business. The actual products or services you offer will merely become a commodity to support the development of your real product and passion, an Asset of Value. This is the true job of any business owner. Focus on that, get

Failing to Build an Asset of Value

it right, and you can rest assured that you will not end up like Clive. It takes time to build an Asset of Value. Start today, build it right and prevent your Clive moment in the future.

Would've, could've, should've, didn't

Clive was a competent and passionate business owner. He should've had the foresight to avoid his situation and build his business differently. Why didn't he? Clive didn't realise that he was building a job instead of a business until it was too late. The failed sale of his business shone a bright light on this fact. He only became aware that he had failed to build a saleable asset late in his career, after years of investing so much effort and making so many sacrifices. Now he was burdened with regret, one of the worst emotions to live with.

Time had run out for him, but if he had acted sooner, he could have done things differently. While you still have the power to do so, change your fate and build your business into an Asset of Value.

We could say that Clive's failure lay in his inability to know his own limitations and blind spots. We all have blind spots and the trick is to be aware of them. Try the following exercise in order to become aware of your limitations.

1. Draw a circle on a piece of paper. The circle represents all of human knowledge.
2. Think about how much of this knowledge you possess. Draw a wedge in the circle to represent this. List some of the things you would include in this wedge of things you know. For example, 'I

know how to write a blog.'

3. Think about how much human knowledge you don't possess. Draw a wedge in the circle to represent this. List some of the things you would include in this wedge of things you don't know. For example, 'I don't know how to perform heart surgery.'

4. Together, these wedges should comprise no more than, say, 10% of the circle. The rest, the big empty space, represents what you aren't even aware of not knowing. There is so much that we don't know, and shedding our ignorance is our own responsibility. In order to live an empowered life in which we take control over our destiny requires us to be constantly working to increase our knowledge. Failing to do so is not fate; it's a choice, especially now that you are aware of it.

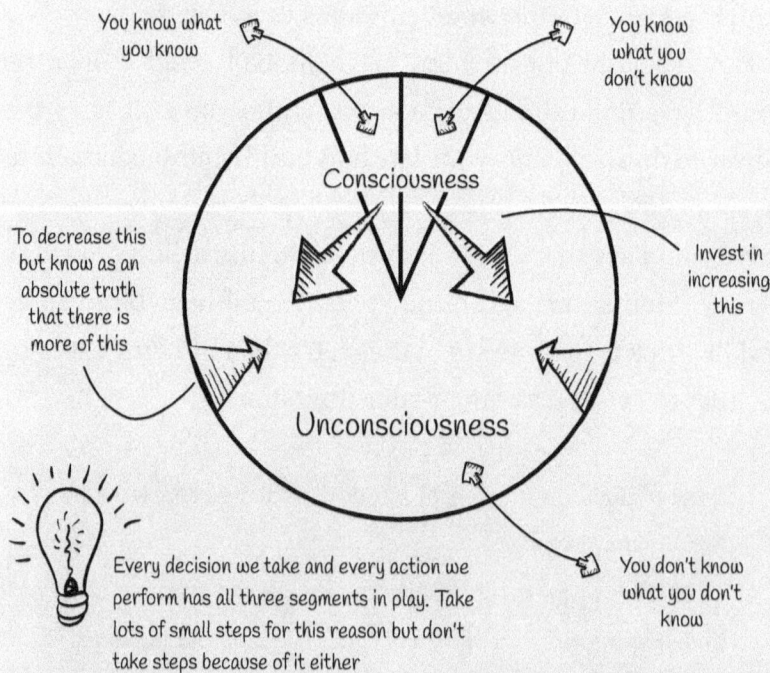

Failing to Build an Asset of Value

We all have unique value. The trick to this short life is to learn what your value is and how it can be of service. To be in service of something more than yourself is where that insight and knowledge of who you are deepen so that you discover your authentic self. Combine that with the courage to act and you will live a life rich with meaning and purpose. Then you will know that nothing is impossible.

- ❏ Ensure that, like Clive, you have an affinity for the sector and industry you are in. Different sectors have different cultures. Ensure that the one you are in resonates with you. If it doesn't, working in that industry will deplete your energy, interest and intelligence in it. Doing anything purely for money is not sustainable.
- ❏ Stick with the sector you enjoy. Persistence in your sector will enable you to build relationships and develop wisdom in your sector that will translate into a constantly improving instinct for what will or won't work.
- ❏ In order to build an Asset of Value, you need to wear two hats. The first is of a shareholder or investor who measures success through increased dividends and capital appreciation. The second is of a director or manager who measures success through increased growth and cashflow.
- ❏ Although you build your business every day for years, you only sell it once. Therefore, get advice on the sale. Your emotions can mislead you in the process of the sale.
- ❏ Carefully consider your decision to sell your business. This should not be taken lightly. Failure to sell for a good price

and on fair terms will erode all of the value you have created. Once you have decided to sell, things will change. You need to ward against taking your foot off the pedal and losing focus.
- When your business revolves around you, and you work so hard every day to simply keep it going, your passion can turn into a slog. We only realise too late that what we have built is not a business that can thrive without us but a job that employs us.
- What you think your business is worth might not be what you will get for it, because your business can't function without you. This is the reality of how your business will be valued, and selling it can come with all sorts of undesirable terms and conditions.
- A sale is not complete until it is paid for. Signing the paperwork is just the first step in the long journey of completing the deal.
- While you still have the power to act, become aware of your limitations and blind spots and change your fate by building your business into one that can work for you.

Chapter 2

A Business is Like a Ship

'Key metaphors help determine what and how we perceive and how we think about our perceptions.' – MH Abrams

At the age of 17, I had no real mind of my own and too much energy that, if not well directed, could have landed me in trouble. At that time in South Africa young men had to perform compulsory military service. I was left with four choices: study further, travel, go to the navy, or go to jail for defying conscription. My parents could not afford the first two options, so I joined the navy and a troublesome journey, but one filled with insight, began. I was a reluctant sailor.

Start with the end in mind
Every journey by sea begins with having a clear destination in mind. Without this, you cannot chart the course, you cannot navigate the ship and you cannot possibly know how much food, fuel and water you will need to get there.

You don't want to be stranded out at sea and to have to explain to your crew that you miscalculated the diesel, food and water requirements and that there are only two days' worth of supplies left. This makes for a horrible end!

Similarly, your business needs a clear destination to sail to. Depending on how well you define your destination, calculate what it will take to get there, and stick to the course you have charted, your business is either going to arrive at the desired port or be stranded. By having a clear end goal for your business in mind you will be able to take the action required today to ensure that you arrive at your destination in future. Constantly changing your destination or being unclear about it greatly increases the probability of ending up lost at sea as your business-building journey comes to an end.

For all businesses, this destination should be that of building an Asset of Value. Your job as the captain of the ship is to keep your business pointed in the right direction at all times. Having a clear destination will help you manage the many challenges of the open seas, guiding your efforts while eliminating the uncertainty of where you are headed. Your destination should never change, in spite of the challenges you will encounter. This requires resilience, grit and hard work.

Purpose determines design

Every ship is built for a specific purpose. This purpose ultimately determines the ship's size, form and dimensions.

I sailed on two different types of ships: Strike Craft and Minehunters. Strike Craft are attack vessels built in Israel, carrying missiles, guns and cannons. They were designed to

A Business is Like a Ship

move fast, with a deep V-shaped hull that cut easily through the water.

Minehunters, designed and built in Germany, have flat, wooden hulls, and are used to detect mines under the water. They were quiet and slow, originally designed to service security interests in Germany's biggest rivers.

Both Strike Craft and Minehunters are designed for flat, calm waters. This made sailing them in the tempestuous seas of the Indian and Atlantic Oceans terrifying. Both of these oceans are characterised by wild seas, big winds and storms and huge swells. I remember being 150 nautical miles due south of Cape Agulhas, three days into a nameless hurricane with swells reaching 10 metres in height. I think you always remember the things that almost killed you.

There are two advantages of designing a ship to optimise its performance. Firstly, it will make the ship more efficient and economical to sail. Secondly, it will make the ship fit for its purpose. For example, the Minehunter, with its wooden hull and super-quiet engines, was designed to make as little noise as possible in order to detect and get closer to underwater mines using sophisticated sonar equipment. Its hull was perfect for sailing in rivers, as was the placement of its propellers, which allowed for tight turns in narrow bodies of water.

The business you build must similarly be designed to optimise its performance. Technically, we call this a business model, which needs to be designed in a particular manner to suit the sector or industry you are in. Your business model includes all the activities you perform daily, from buying to operations to sales. The extent to which these are organised and coordinated determines how effective your business model design is. These fundamentals are crucial to get right, otherwise expect a very rough, bumpy and costly ride.

Where you spend your time determines what you will achieve

My first post was that of a ship engineer in the engine room. The engine room houses enormous diesel engines that drive the propellers. It is located below decks in the hull of the ship and acts as a ballast to stabilise the vessel in oceans that always felt as if they were in flux.

I cannot remember a time when my hands and arms up to my elbows were not covered in grease. The worst part of this job was that I could not see the sea. There are no portholes in the hull and you had very little idea which direction you were sailing in. Seasickness was an almost every-day occurrence. There was a toxic mix of diesel filling your nostrils, deafening engines, and poor light combined with the ceaseless vibrations of the hull fighting the water, guaranteeing seasickness the moment you left a protected port and headed into the open ocean.

I was always busy doing something. The fixing never stopped. The force that the sea exerted on the hull moving through it put tremendous strain on the engines, the propeller shafts and the propellers themselves. I was always running from one issue to the next, spanner in one hand, Q20 lubricant

A Business is Like a Ship

in the other.

The engine room is like the delivery end of a business. It makes things happen. The buying, operational and distribution activities of a business make the business move forward in response to the marketing and sales activities that bring the customers in. It needs to be constantly working and purring to ensure constant forward momentum.

I made sure I paid my dues fast and performed well enough to be invited above decks. *Fresh air at last*, I thought. Thank heavens for it, since my work was physically demanding. But life above decks was a constant hell of maintenance. I remember the hours of scraping barnacles off the ship's hull, sanding and repainting rails and bulkheads and constantly washing, shining and maintaining everything else on that ship.

In harbour, they dressed me up in diving gear and gave me a scrubbing brush to clean the hull. A dirty hull, full of sea life, causes drag on the ship, increasing energy costs and reducing speed.

Like a ship, a business needs to be constantly maintained. Changes to staff, business activities, and communicating with clients and customers, among other things, require constant attention.

Carien and I learned this fast. One of the businesses we built, a Wireless Application Service Provider (WASP), which sold ringtones, wallpapers and content in the early years of mobile phones in South Africa, grew in revenue from zero to more than R25m a month in just three years. It was a monster that needed constant maintenance. Almost every month we had to break down and rebuild elements of the business to keep it from hitting speed wobbles.

As any business grows its operations increase in complexity that if not managed will turn into chaos. You know you have reached this point if you feel you have hit a ceiling of growth and you are struggling to break through to the next level.

Eventually, I was invited to join the leadership team on the ship's bridge. The bridge is the highest point on a ship and houses the navigation room, with a 270-degree view of the ocean, padded seats, a dashboard of instruments and a Nespresso machine. It was a great place to be.

On the bridge, I had different responsibilities. One of these was to lead the planning of our seafaring journeys. I was responsible for determining the amount of food, fuel and water required for our voyages. If we set sail from Durban to Mumbai, for example, we would be at sea for 12 days, and being smart, we would plan to take 15 days' worth of supplies in case things went wrong. A business, too, needs a resource plan to get you from where you are to where you are going. This means a clear destination and a plan supported by a budget.

With our destination clearly set and our course charted, we used instruments to check the weather we would be sailing into, and we used the controls to either sail through or around the storms and currents. We were in control and we shouted the orders down to the crew in the engine rooms. My main job on the bridge was to constantly point the ship towards the destination. I had to ensure that the forward momentum created in the engine room translated into the ship arriving at port.

Where are you spending your time in your business? You can only be in control if you are spending your time on the ship's bridge. Given that you take all the risks and are the most expensive resource in your business, shouldn't you be leading and directing the ship from the bridge rather than working in the engine room? If you stay in the engine room, like Clive did, you will be building a job. It's from the bridge that you ensure that the business you are building will become an Asset of Value.

Get the right people to do the right thing at the right time
Unless you are sailing a small boat, it is impossible to do everything, all the time, to keep your business operating smoothly. This is a recipe for remaining a micro business. Growth brings complexity, and the larger the ship, the more vital it is that you have a good crew to help you sail it.

A ship's crew is made up of people with varying skills and responsibilities. There's the captain, and there are the first and second mates, the navigators, engineers, cooks, deckhands and so on. Each is trained to perform a specific role. For example, a ship's engineers excel at maintaining the diesel engines but are lousy navigators and cooks. Getting the right people to do the right thing at the right time in your business is one of the most important factors in building an Asset of Value.

This is something that has contributed to much of our

success at Aurik. We often work with business owners who, out of comfort, expedience or simply ignorance, choose the wrong person for the job. For example, an owner might make their top-performing salesperson sales manager in spite of that employee lacking the skills to manage a team. This seldom ends well for anyone.

Every business needs a set of standard operating procedures

An enormously valuable lesson I learned from my time in the navy was the importance of adhering to standard operating procedures. For example, when sailing a 500-ton vessel into port, skipping a single procedure could result in disaster. Such a large ship sailing at 10 kilometres per hour into another craft would cause extensive damage. Following operating procedures conscientiously, from passage or voyage plans to equipment checks and a host of other things, meant I only had one accident under my command.

Sticking to procedures results in each of the crew knowing exactly what to do, when to do it and how to do it. This makes delegation easier and builds trust among the crew.

A business should also have a set of standard operating procedures. This creates predictability and certainty, and results in better organisation for staff, customers and suppliers. Following a clear plan also lets you spend more time on the bridge rather than in the engine room. It lets you direct the business with a greater degree of certainty and confidence.

The lack of standard operating procedures in Clive's business led to his failure to make a clean sale. Without these guidelines, the buyer argued, they were buying a ship that only the business owner knew how to sail.

Where you spend your time will shape the ship you build
As a business owner, where do you spend most of your time? In the engine room, putting out fires, or on the bridge, guiding the direction and growth of your business? Most business owners spend their time in the engine room. The business drives the owner as opposed to the owner driving the business. This is because the business is poorly built, creating chaos in operations and requiring the owner to be constantly fixing and rejigging the engine room. As a result, these owners are not able to spot the next big opportunity or avoid storms that could sink their business. It is only from the bridge that you can direct the ship, set the course and ensure you arrive at your destination, offload your cargo and get paid.

The open sea is full of surprises. Waves, wind, currents and storms bash the ship and threaten its safe passage. The business environment is no different. Every day we face political regulation that impedes business, volatile currency fluctuations, uncertain energy supply and hectic competition. As business owners, we should find comfort in this. It's never personal. These storms threaten every business, regardless of who you are. Recognising when a storm could rise up and planning for it is the practice of foresight. How often do you think about future events that you will face in your business? If you do, you are already a few steps ahead of your competitors.

❏ Building and operating a business is like constructing and sailing a ship. Its size, crew and systems must be carefully considered if you are to arrive at your destination.
❏ You need to design and build your business to be fit for purpose. This will ensure it operates optimally and economically. In order to get this right, you will need to constantly redesign and rebuild it.
❏ As the captain of your ship, you need to set a clear course for your business. Your destination should be to build an Asset of Value.
❏ You should be leading and directing your ship from the bridge rather than spending your time in the engine room, constantly putting out fires. You can only be in control from the bridge, where you have access to data and instruments that will allow you to spot opportunities and threats and monitor the ship's performance.
❏ Where you spend your time every day will determine if you are simply creating a job for yourself or building an Asset of Value. The more time you spend in the engine room, the more likely it is that you are just manufacturing a job for yourself.
❏ You need a good crew to help you sail your vessel.
❏ Having standard operating procedures for your business will make it clear for everyone what their job is. This creates

certainty and results in better organisation. It also lets you spend more time on the bridge, managing your ship. By creating these operating procedures, you will empower your crew to be the best they can be, so that you can also be at your best in leading the business and taking it to the next level.

Chapter 3

Defining an Asset of Value

'If one does not know to which port one is sailing, no wind is favourable.' – Lucius Annaeus Seneca

It is clear that passion is not enough to succeed in business. Clive had it in bucket loads. Yet he failed to build his business into one that could be sold at a fair price and without punishing terms and conditions.

What was Clive missing? His time spent solving technical problems and delivering his service to his customers could have been better spent building systems to enable the smooth operation of his business. In order to build an Asset of Value, a business owner needs to purposely build her or his business from the start into one that can generate revenue without the owner being directly involved in the daily operations. We call this a business's System of Delivery. For example, Clive could have spent more time hiring the right people to do the work for him and developing a set of operational procedures, practices and guidelines for his staff to follow. These systems must be built across the business,

Defining An Asset Of Value

from operations to accounting, human resources, marketing and sales.

Clive's business operated as a result of his product knowledge and customer engagement, meaning that Clive *was* the business. His purpose should have been less about the actual services and products he offered and more about the way his business was designed. He also focused too narrowly on the actual services and products he offered instead of on the particular problems his business solved for his customers.

Clive tended to offer new products as the solution to the problems his customers experienced. For example, when their documents failed to print due to poor network connectivity, requiring Clive's staff to be called out to reboot the router, Clive would suggest his clients purchase a new, updated router to improve the connection. But his clients were reluctant to pay for this. If Clive had interpreted the customer's frustration in business as opposed to product-feature terms, he could have identified an opportunity to solve his customers' problem by charging them for printing instead of hardware. This would have reduced Clive's cost in doing call-outs, ensured smooth connectivity and reduced his clients' hassle, saving them time and money.

How then do we define an Asset of Value?
An Asset of Value is a business that demonstrates the following features:
- It solves well-defined, quantifiable problems for specific types of customers through tailor-made experiences. This

distinguishes it from other businesses in a competitive market;
- It has as its foundation a solid System of Delivery. This comprises systems for all of the functions of the business, including marketing, sales, operations, procurement, accounting and human resources. These systems are made up of activities organised into a logical sequence, with clearly defined operating procedures. They have been built to solve customer problems and deliver specific customer experiences, and they generate leads and convert sales to ensure the business's momentum;
- Its systems are operated by a purposeful team – the right people who do the right thing at the right time. This team is empowered to act with confidence and certainty in a manner that fulfils the business's positioning and purpose;
- It is run by a leader who spends at least 60% of his or her time on the bridge, where he or she can focus on accelerating its growth and value, generating more cashflow and funds;
- It is a business that will appeal to funders and financers because it is designed in such a way that they will be confident to invest money into its growth, with a high degree of certainty that they will get a return on their investment; and finally
- It is a business that, should you choose to sell it one day, will fetch a premium price and a fair deal. This places you, the owner, in a position where you will have options regarding buyers and the terms of the deal.

Defining an Asset of Value

In the drawing below, I have captured the seven activities that build an Asset of Value. They are worth keeping in mind. Make a copy and stick it on your office door, computer screen and toilet door. What you think about has a huge impact on what you do!

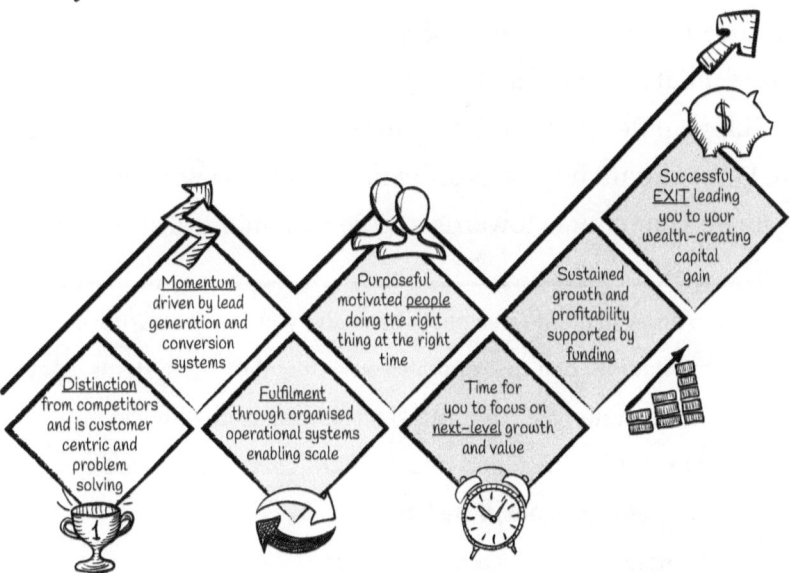

At Aurik we currently work with 504 established businesses whose owners have each invested over 45 000 hours in total into their businesses. Surely this time and energy needs to be rewarded. Achieving success directly depends on how you build your business today. It is not subject to fate, hope and prayers. It is completely in your hands.

You can't control the wind but you can adjust your sails

Business owners often ask me, given the turbulent times we live in, 'How often should my business strategy change?'

When building an Asset of Value, the path you take to reach your destination port will undoubtedly change due to unpredictable seas, storms, wind and currents. You will either sail through or around them. Sometimes you will take shelter from these storms. You need to find the shortest, least risky path. You can only do this from the bridge of your ship and if you have reliable instruments on your dashboard.

But your destination should never change. Building an Asset of Value should be your North Star, which you will use to navigate on your course towards a more certain, rewarding future.

- ❏ In order to create a saleable business, you need to purposely build it into one that operates smoothly through systems.
- ❏ These systems – from marketing to sales, operations, procurement, money and people – are collectively called the business's **System of Delivery**.
- ❏ An Asset of Value is a business that:
    - Is **positioned** to solve problems for customers;
    - Has a solid **System of Delivery**;
    - Is run by a motivated and capable **team**;
    - Is run by a leader who directs it from the bridge, with **time** to focus on **accelerating growth**;
    - Is primed to **innovate**; and
    - Can one day be sold for a good price and on favourable terms.
- ❏ While the path you take to get to your destination will undoubtedly change due to the challenges you will face along the way, your destination should never change. Building an

Defining an Asset of Value

Asset of Value should be your North Star.

❏ Achieving success is not subject to fate. It is completely in your hands.

Chapter 4

Building an Asset of Value

'Systems help us to move forward, to go as far as we possibly can. They enable us to work faster, smarter, and more strategically. A good system eliminates waste, while it also anticipates and removes obstacles.' – John Maxwell

Who really cares about us private business owners?

We are told that the government cares about us. Often politicians and bureaucrats say things like, 'SMBs are the backbone of the economy and the engines of job creation.' The numbers corroborate this: nearly two-thirds of all private-sector jobs in South Africa are generated by SMBs.[2] Our politicians encourage us to start businesses, become entrepreneurs and grow our businesses to support the jobs and economic prosperity of the country. But these words of encouragement are empty. We build our businesses in a policy environment devoid of any useful, workable incentives. Commitments – such as paying SMB suppliers on time, reducing red tape for SMBs and passing legislation to ensure a fairer playing field and legal rights of SMBs – remain misguided and empty.

Building an Asset of Value

Corporations and multinational companies emphasise our importance in creating jobs and a stable customer base. We bring innovation to the industries we work in and create acquisition opportunities for these large companies. But corporations often pay us late for our services and products, compete unfairly and poach our ideas and talent.

Labour unions love us because we generate revenue for them and give them reasons to exist, but they feel antagonised by us, claiming we are hard to organise as workers.

The media loves us because we create opportunities for compelling content in reality shows or inspiring books, articles and movies. Our suppliers and employees hopefully appreciate us because we generate opportunities for them.

Finally, our families value us because we create security, opportunities and stability for them to fulfil their dreams. But even this value is aligned more to their personal interests and insecurities than our needs as business owners. I have sat with clients at countless lunch and dinner tables discussing the hard work and sacrifices required for a family business to thrive.

Ultimately, it is you who really cares about your business. Your actions and choices alone will determine the success or failure of your business. It's a brutal but true idea that you, and only you, are responsible for your business and the future you create for it. You are the only captain of your ship.

Jack, an Asset of Value builder

I first met Jack a year after we opened Aurik for business. Jack was 54 and wanted to sell the bakery business he had started at

29. He would become a lighthouse to the ship we were building at Aurik. He would warn us of danger, share his journey, ask our advice and challenge it, and through his actions we received constant feedback regarding what worked and what didn't when it came to building an Asset of Value (though we would only coin the term 'Asset of Value' later, when I met Themba, who was in the business of pumping waste water for the gold mines). Jack gave of his opinions and advice freely and introduced me to many people.

At the time, Carien and I, with our partners, had just completed listing a human-resources business on the JSE. The listing had gone well, with demand for our shares exceeding availability by 400%. While this was flattering, it was not a good result. It meant that our pre-listing share price was undervalued. Yet, the market loved the idea of what this business could be. I had worked with five others to pull this business together and the value of a well-balanced, motivated team was evident in the final result.

Word spread of our success and people's interest in what we did was growing. Jack had heard about it, too, and he contacted me for help. We scheduled the first meeting with him at our offices. By then, we had moved out of the stationery cupboard into offices of our own. Our big wooden table, the one that had protruded out the room into the corridor at the architect's office, now had its own room – our boardroom. It created just the impression we wanted, along with the rest of our work space, seeming to resonate with the payoff line that we had developed for Aurik: 'People, Ideas and Action.'

Building an Asset of Value

We met in the boardroom. Jack, a big, burly, heavyset man with a beard, arrived and we shook hands. He had broad, heavy hands – hands that were equally deft with pen and tool. He sat down at the head of the table while I sat to the side.

Jack was only our second client after the chicken farmer who we had built the incubators for. We hadn't even developed a system for engaging with business owners at that stage. We were still figuring out what we did.

'So, Jack, how's business today?' I began nervously.

He looked at me, taking in my measure, deciding if he could trust me. I knew I was going to be tested.

'We generate almost R55m a year,' he answered, looking me directly in the eye.

That, during the mid-2000s, was a sizeable private business. I swallowed, hoping he wouldn't notice. He had a powerful presence. *What the hell is he doing here?* I caught myself thinking for a brief moment.

'Really? So, what do you do?' was all I could come up with in response.

'I'm a baker,' he answered.

A baker, doing that kind of revenue? I started to relax. In my earlier days in business, I had acquired a bakery on behalf of a client. It was a biscuit-maker that used three fully automated ovens that operated nearly 24 hours a day to produce 62 tons of biscuits a month. It was a sizable business that I managed to sell for R88m to a listed company. I was sure Jack noticed I had relaxed. He smiled briefly.

'I'm here,' he offered, 'because I can't sell my business. I've had it on the market for two years but can't get the price I want.'

This was a position I would hear many times in the future. His story was interesting. At least, I found it interesting – but then again, I find everyone's story interesting. Baking was in Jack's blood. His dad had been a baker. After living at home with his family, Jack studied toward a commercial degree at a recognised university. He then went to work in corporate bakeries before opening his own business.

I love stories like this. I admire business owners who have stayed the course in the sector or industry they are in. They have a deep understanding of their business, long relationships with their customers and suppliers, good reputations and many ideas. I love the fact that the world is forever changing and through that change something that once worked might not be relevant today, meaning there are always opportunities for new people, even in an old industry. People like Jack have seen so much, tried so many different things, and make for the material of a great business.

Trying to be everything to everyone makes you nothing to no one

'What exactly do you do?' I asked Jack.

He came to life. We were on his favourite subject – his business; his first love; the thing he ate, breathed and dreamed. Jack's time was taken up by a number of business activities. He had two big silos, which he would fill with 20 tons of flour every week. He would use this to fill 25kg and 50kg bags,

Building an Asset of Value

which he would deliver to all the small bakeries within a few hundred kilometres of his location.

He had also imported the Macadams Baking System from Holland, one of the best in the world. It consisted of ovens, mixers and everything his customers needed to become expert bakers. Jack sold, installed and serviced this fool-proof system in SPAR grocery stores – the same franchise that we see today all over the country – which needed freshly baked goods every day to serve their morning customers.

An innovator by nature with a long history in the baking game, Jack was the first person in South Africa to commercialise a concept that today is common practice. He combined a coffee shop and bakery into one store. It was genius: one lease, two sets of foot traffic.

Jack also supplied baked breakfast goods such as croissants, buns and brioches, and high-tea confectioneries such as cakes, sweet pastries, doughnuts, scones, and cookies to hotel groups.

His eyes lit up, his energy lifted, and his normally heavy presence was light and energetic. He loved the idea of his business. He loved his products even more. He boasted that his croissants were the best in the country, if not the world, and that the recipe was his father's.

I, on the other hand, was exhausted. I looked more closely at Jack and behind his now-buoyant energy I saw a 154-year-old man. The complexity of his business left me with a headache and in dismay. The problem lay bare: too many ideas in one business; too much activity to manage; too complicated for anyone to want to buy; and too much in Jack's head.

'Anything else?' I asked sardonically.

'Actually, yes,' he sneered.

This way of speaking to each other set the tone for our future engagements for years to come.

'For the last five years, we haven't been able to crack more than R55 million. Our numbers are bouncing between R50 million and R55 million and it feels like we have hit a glass ceiling,' he said, sitting back and folding his arms. He looked at me challengingly.

I asked Jack to leave me with his numbers from the last two years and said I'd get back to him.

The ceiling of complexity

Jack's numbers screamed out 'sine wave'! The drawing here illustrates how the ceiling of complexity keeps you out of your business's engine room.

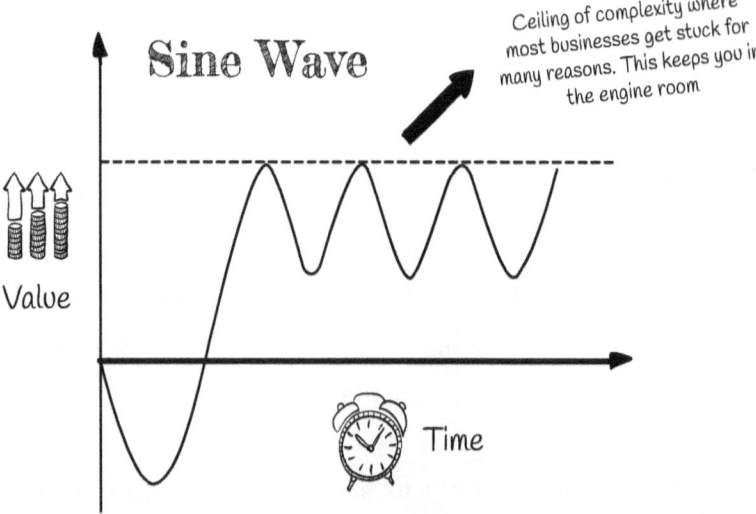

Building an Asset of Value

A sine wave is a neat, continuous wave that rises and falls, moving from left to right. Jack's numbers told the tale of someone caught in something my colleague Marcus calls 'the ceiling of complexity', in which your revenue goes up and down in a continuous wave without being able to breach a certain limit. There you are, selling hard, you win a deal and money comes in – the rise of the wave. Then you work hard and incur expenses to service the sale – the fall of the wave. Once done, you endlessly repeat the process without any overall growth in the amount of money you are making.

This is the nemesis of most business owners. Being caught in this cycle is like being stuck in the engine room of your ship – you work hard to maintain the business and propel it forward but fail to grow it.

Jack's croissants, the 'best in the world' by his reckoning, were stalled en route to new markets because he was trapped in a sine-wave cycle of sell, service and repeat, pinning him and his business down. Snapping out of this cycle was key to his growth and vital in building an Asset of Value. Who would want to buy Jack's business if they knew it was trapped in a sine-wave pattern, confined by a ceiling of complexity? This is a key reason why so many business that survive their first five years are never sold.

Data is gold

Numbers, or data, are gold if you respect and use them well. Data, in the form of GPS coordinates and the indicators on the many dials on the bridge's dashboard, gives the captain of a ship clarity when sailing in a fog. I am reminded of my time working with David, a machine-learning expert, former actuary, and an exceptionally gifted mathematician who I was working with on building a software program that used psychometrics to evaluate the fundability of a business owner based on her or his personality.

David continually frustrated me with his pedantic insistence on analysis. A devout man, he always remained perfectly calm in our exchanges. I wanted to get our product to market, but we disagreed on the final price of it and his lack of urgency infuriated me.

'Sometimes you have to go with what you have, David,' I said to him. 'Trust me, we'll see what works and what doesn't and adjust the price accordingly. We have to get cash flowing!'

Calmly, he looked at me. He then raised his hand above his head and placed it on his yarmulke and said, 'Pavlo, in God I trust, for the rest, give me data!'

While I am yet to meet a business owner who has built her or his business in order to create back-office systems, it is these systems, which generate and run on data, that prevent disaster. Data removes the noise around and the emotions involved in decisions; it reveals patterns from the past that you can use to control your business's future; and critically, it supports your business's valuation if and when you decide to sell it. Digitising your business systems and activities will enable you to build your business and improve its value. This will allow you to scale your business. For this reason, data has become indispensable for every business owner.

- As business owners, it's only us who really care about our businesses. Therefore, it's up to us to take control and be the captain of our own ship.
- Serving every customer and opportunity that crosses your path will result in a lack of clarity in what you do and cause chaos in your operations.
- This can result in your business hitting what is called a **ceiling of complexity** in which you work hard to maintain your chaotic business without ever growing it.
- As a result, your revenue will take the shape of a **sine-wave pattern**, rising as money comes in from winning a deal and falling as you incur expenses to service the deal, with the cycle endlessly repeating.
- Data can be very useful in helping you figure out if you have become trapped in a cycle of sell, service and repeat, indicating that you need to find a way to grow your business out of this pattern.

Chapter 5

Purpose and Positioning

'Set your course by the stars. Not by the lights of every passing ship.' – Omar Bradley

Jack and I agreed to work together, and so a long journey of business building began. I was excited that Carien and I had our first real client and the Aurik we wanted to build was becoming a reality.

Six weeks into our relationship, sitting in our boardroom, Jack and I had a fight. I argued that his business was too complicated and I was insistent that to simplify it he must select only one group of customers to serve. He was either to sell flour to his small-bakery customers, continue to supply the hotel groups with confectioneries and baked goods, or focus on his coffee shop-bakery stores.

My reasoning was simple. 'When you try to be all things to everyone, you become nothing to no one,' I explained. 'We need to re-evaluate your business's positioning. We need to figure out what makes your business truly special and narrow your focus on that.'

Purpose and Positioning

We couldn't rely on what he considered to be superior products and service in order to position his business well. Any of his competitors could supply great products and deliver excellent services, and they could compete on price at any time. These things did not make Jack's business special enough in comparison with his competitors. Until we got this right, any work we did towards building an Asset of Value would have been in vain.

Jack was reluctant to give up some of his customers, but I persisted, and what I had thought was a debate turned into an argument that quickly escalated into a fight.

In a fury, Jack slammed his fist down on the table and stormed out. My table split one-third up its length, the chair he'd sat on fell over, and Jack was gone. My nerves were shattered.

Maybe the business books were right after all, and I was wrong. Perhaps the customer *is* always right and perhaps the customer really *is* king, and I should have agreed with Jack not to get rid of some of his customers. But as I sat there and thought more about it, I realised my passion for business and commitment to the principles we were developing had guided me in advising Jack. Irrespective of what the business is and who the owner is, I always see the potential in both. That's the benefit of loving what you do and believing in it: you develop a positive approach to everything you do. Being clear about how a business should be designed and built turns that positivity into confident, clear actions that are authentic to yourself and your work.

My passionate belief that a business must be built into an

Asset of Value is a great example of purpose. Purpose is different from your business's positioning in that it is personal; it is what motivates you. Your purpose talks to why you do what you do. It generates meaning in your work and that, in turn, creates the source of your passion, the fuel you need to endure the journey of building a business. A clearly defined purpose draws people with similar values to your business, be they employees, suppliers or customers. It creates an authenticity that, because you originate it, makes you distinct from others. Brought to life through action, your purpose animates your brand.

I was saddened by the loss of our very first, real client, and I felt terrible. I had an obligation to Carien to land our first clients. But my private pity party was interrupted two minutes later as I sat in the boardroom looking at our cracked table, reflecting on what had happened, when I heard a commotion at reception. Jack had returned and he stormed into the boardroom. I jumped up from my seat and assumed a defensive stance. I have been involved in martial arts most of my life and it was instinctual. Still in a fury, Jack grabbed the toppled chair and sat down and barked at me: 'F*** you, I'll do it!'

Change is the key to opportunity

We decided to narrow our focus to the hotel groups. South Africa was in the halo of its democracy dividend. Tourism was booming and going to boom further. We learned that a number of international hotel groups had big plans to develop more hotels around the country. It seemed like the local currency would weaken, and this would boost tourism further. At the time, South African Tourism had a very capable CEO whose strategy and ability to deploy it was promising.

The first year went by quickly and an enormous amount of work had been done. Jack sold his silos off and ceased supplying flour to his small-bakery clients. It had only earned low profit margins, in any event. He had to compete on price for his products, and in order to get his price right, he had to buy in greater quantity. His small profit was also being consumed by the costs of maintaining a growing fleet of trucks and paying drivers.

Jack also sold three of his four coffee shop-bakery stores, admitting that he was relieved to do so. Retail consumers can be very difficult to please and are extremely vocal in expressing their dissatisfaction. Added to this, Jack had to deal with the constant problem of unreliable staff.

He sold the Macadams Baking System, although he insisted on finding a good buyer for it. This was the toughest one for Jack to let go of. The relationships he had established with the supplier in Holland and his grocery-store clients meant a lot to him. Jack always went the extra mile for his grocery-store clients, who loved him. Grocers are in a tough, competitive, 365-days-a-year business. They source thousands of perishable and non-perishable goods from many different suppliers. Missing a beat in this game means missing your monthly profit numbers and this means money out of pocket. The earliest relationships we form with our customers, especially in the business-to-business environment, are the toughest ones to transform or end as your business finds its feet. However, it was a good move for Jack. It freed up the large amount of money that had gone into paying for spare parts and service technicians, which was needed to meet the requirements of Macadams, and Jack's supply agreements with the grocery stores were extensive.

At the end of the year, Jack called a meeting. We sat at my now mostly repaired table. He slid his end-of-year financial reports across the table to me and asked, 'What do you think?'

Tentatively, I turned the first page and quickly scanned the income statement. A tiny bead of sweat appeared on my forehead as I noticed that we had broken a record. For the first time in five years, Jack's business had generated *less* than R50m turnover. It was a complete collapse in revenue.

I looked up quickly; I could feel his eyes on me. His face remained expressionless but his eyes, no, they were neither angry nor frustrated; they were smiling ever so slightly. I looked at the profit percentage. It had stayed the same, give or take a couple of points, as the number for the previous year! As I looked up at Jack, he smiled broadly. My relief was palpable as I smiled in return. We had reshaped his business into one that was simpler, less chaotic, easier to manage, and cleaner to build.

Your business needs to be customer-led

What had we learned? When starting a new business, serve whoever walks through your door, regardless of who they are. It could be a chicken farmer looking for incubators or a Jack looking for help to grow his business differently. This is vital because you need cashflow. However, always remember that your idea for your business and what you want it to be is really all about you. If the customer is king, does that mean you need to be the customer's slave? I think not!

We also learned that research and business models offer ideas, but they are not silver bullets. You will learn more by engaging with your customers. Ask them what they like and don't like. Push them for their feelings rather than their thoughts. Learn how to listen to and hear what people are saying. Watch them. What they do is more revealing than what they say about how they feel.

Your job is to see who these people are and how they are responding to your idea wrapped in a business. When customers start to repeat-buy and refer friends, look closely at what they are repeat-buying and referring. Is it the product, service, experience, price, location or environment – what is it exactly that they like? The key to building a business and unlocking its potential is that it must be customer-led. In the early days, it is your idea that leads the business. Over time, if your customers' needs don't become the driving force of the business, you are going to travel a rough road, one that will wear you down.

As iron sharpens iron, one person sharpens another
Jack was re-energised. I was thrilled. At Aurik, Carien and I were building the lessons we learned into what would become our Asset of Value approach, adding them to what we had learned

ourselves in the businesses we had started, built and sold.

Today, having worked with nearly 2 000 entrepreneurial business owners across four continents, I still walk away from each engagement learning so much more than what I knew coming into it. We work hard to constantly improve our approach and structure of engaging and working with business owners, integrating every bit of new learning into our method, to translate action into results.

Before I sat down in my office to deal with my emails, the phone rang. It was Jack. He sounded nervous.

'We have a problem,' he said. 'The market is not responding fast enough to the new direction of my business.'

This was serious. 'What's happening, Jack?' I asked.

The data supported his concerns. The hotel groups preferred to be contacted about promotions via email. Every month, Jack was sending out promotional emails to about 60 hotel groups responsible for around 1 500 hotels in South Africa. The response rate from his customers was 9.8% to 14.7%, depending on the season. Of those, he converted 34.8% into sales, a high number in the greater scheme of things. These deals were significant enough to build a reasonable business, but Jack wanted more. We agreed to meet. What emerged was a key insight into building a business into an Asset of Value.

Specialise to stand out from the crowd

What makes your business special? What gives you a distinct advantage over your competitors?

When I first met Jack, he believed that his superior croissants gave him an edge over his competitors. He believed that by supplying his customers the best croissants he was solving all of their needs, resulting in his business's particular specialisation.

But specialisation cannot be defined by your product or service alone. While you might be offering the best product or service today, your suppliers could provide better ones tomorrow. The most that Jack's knowledge of baking and his superior croissants would ever get him was a compliment. What we were really after was specialisation resulting in annuity revenues – regular, predictable income as opposed to earnings from once-off deals.

Instead, specialisation comes from creating sustained value for your customers. This value must be defined by your customers, not you. It must be measurable, not anecdotal. Customers define value by the quality of the experience you have given them in solving their problems. The product you sell to a customer is only part of this experience.

Identifying the problems that you solve for customers entails awareness of your customers' needs, engagement with your customers, and contemplating opportunities in delivery and after-care. It also needs to factor in the customer's experience. Quality results from experience. A beautiful product accompanied by a terrible buying experience or service creates bitterness. We have all felt this. The experience a customer has in working with your business defines their impression of it. It also determines their behaviour. In a flash, customers will communicate a bad experience to the world through social media. They might not do the same for a good experience, but a positive interaction will bring that customer back repeatedly.

Consider this example. Imagine that a pipe bursts in your bathroom. You call a plumber to fix it. The plumber knows what he is doing and fixes the problem, but he leaves a mess of handprints on the walls, copper shavings on the floor and he chips your mirror while carrying his toolbox out the bathroom. The next time you have a plumbing problem, you call another plumber who also knows what he is doing and fixes the problem. Afterwards, he also cleans up. Which plumber are you likely to call back in future?

Businesses that understand what customer experience ought to be like and deliver it consistently are better positioned than their competitors. This goes beyond skill, technical knowledge and products.

Knowing first who your customer of choice is and then creating the time to understand their lived reality keeps you ahead of their problems and desired experiences. This makes for a resilient business.

There is time and money involved in every interaction. True specialisation includes a comprehensive, holistic understanding of the sum total of these elements.

The fundamental problem that Jack's business was solving was not the need for excellent croissants but rather a business need. For example, providing additional confectionery products to a coffee shop wanting to distinguish itself from its competitors. This goes well beyond the croissant recipe.

Replace product-feature solutions with problem-solving ones

Jack always told me that baking a croissant right every time was not a simple task. A good croissant is crispy on the outside, chewy on the inside and is almost hollow to the touch, making it feel light. It has a very particular mouth feel, and eating one makes you want to eat another. There is a science to food production. I believed him; they were delicious. He spoke extensively about his proprietary recipes and manufacturing processes, intellectual property that he had paid a lot in study fees to develop and which he guarded closely. Why, Jack wondered, given his proven methods as well as his relationships and experience, could he not ramp up sales?

Whenever I asked Jack what customer problem he solved for the hotel groups, he gave the same answer: 'I supply them with fresh, delicious products produced with unique recipes, and I go the extra mile for them, providing reliable service.'

Jack always took a product-centric position. Nothing he said spoke to the positioning an Asset of Value needs: solving a well-articulated customer problem through a very particular experience!

I suggested we visit some customers together. Perhaps a fresh perspective, rather than a fresh croissant, was needed.

Jack's predicament was similar to that of another client, Ismail, a watch-shop owner who Carien and I would meet later at a time when our Asset of Value method was more developed and we better knew how to prompt business owners to identify their specialisation. In Ismail's case, finding out what made his business special was as simple as asking, 'What makes you special in your customers' eyes?' This allowed us to identify the problems that Ismail solved for his customers and to reshape his business to win a difficult retail environment.

Ismail – What problems do you solve for your customers?

Ismail owned a watch shop, which he had inherited from his father. The shop was in a busy mall, where he had been for many years. He stocked only the best, most expensive, top-brand watches. The average price of a watch in Ismail's shop was R380k. His tenure in the business provided his customers with confidence of purchase.

If someone were to ask one of Ismail's customers where they got their watch from, they would likely reply, 'If you're looking for a top-end watch, go to Ismail. He knows his stuff and they have been there forever.'

At our first meeting with Ismail, I asked him, 'What is the single-biggest problem you face in your business?'

'Sales have declined since 2008,' Ismail began. 'At first I thought it was the tough economy, because customers are negotiating harder on price than ever before. But then I realised this isn't true because my clients aren't too affected by the economy. They are wealthy people.' He paused for a moment, thinking through his answer. 'Maybe it's also because digital watches are coming in so there has been a small drop-off in demand for my watches, although it hasn't

Purpose and Positioning

been significant. Or maybe because I'm Indian customers expect to trade and bargain with me.'

None of these reasons were plausible for the decline in his business.

'What makes you special in your customers' eyes, Ismail?' I asked next.

'Our range of watches,' Ismail replied. 'We get the limited editions of the top brands in the world. Each brand makes an allocation of limited editions for various countries, and we are first on the list for South Africa. Also, we have been around for a long time, so people know we are here and will be here tomorrow. That certainty gives them confidence to buy from us, knowing that we have genuine articles, and should there be any problems, we will make it right.'

It was a good proposition but a product- and service-centric proposition none the less. I wanted to dig deeper. 'What problems do you solve for your customers?'

'Hey man, Pavlo, my customers don't know what problems are. They are very wealthy individuals,' he laughed in reply.

'I'm not convinced,' I retorted. 'Let's do some work to understand who buys these expensive watches so that we can better understand what drives the purchase, Ismail. That will form the basis of our next move to get sales up to where you think they should be in this economy.'

Over a period of three months of engaging customers, we worked with Ismail to classify them into four distinct groups: the Collectors, the Investors, the Launderers and the VIPs. Ismail coined the terms and defined them further. Collectors invest in brand names, such as Rolex, for example, and watches designed for particular activities, such as sailing or diving watches. They collect across brands over time. Investors look for portable value: watches that can be bought in one country and easily sold in another. Launderers buy and sell watches within short periods of time in order to wash undeclared income to avoid paying taxes. Finally, VIPs want a watch to make an overt statement of having arrived. These were four very different types of customers. Ismail had intuitively known this but never invested in understanding it to this extent.

In defining the customer groups, we had identified the problems that Ismail solved for each of them. It was a good start. We developed a series of sales activities and scripts to suit the needs of each of these customer groups and trained Ismail's staff in selling watches to each group. When a customer came into the shop looking to buy a watch, the sales representative would ask her or him two friendly questions and use the customer's response to place her or him into one of the four customer groups.

The rest of the sales interaction was designed to create a particular experience for the customer based on which group he or she fell into. The watch would be selected, presented and displayed in order to bolster this experience. For example, the VIP would be told upon presenting the watch in question, 'Interestingly, sir, the most recent acquisition of this watch was by [for example] Prince Harry or Jeff Bezos,' and with that, the sales representative would show the customer a picture of the said celebrity wearing the watch. That entire engagement resonated with the psychology of the VIP customer. In feeling heard and understood, the customer's confidence and trust motivating a purchase grew. The same watch elicited three different engagements with customers who fitted into the remaining

Purpose and Positioning

> customer groups.
>
> Since 2010, Ismail has consistently enjoyed a 28.3% compound annual growth rate. He has achieved this in a global recession with a luxury product!
>
> A well-positioned business solves well-articulated problems for well-defined customer groups through a well-crafted experience. The extent to which you can quantify the problem you are solving for your customer is the extent to which you have defined, understood and measured the problem.

Ask and you will be served

Jack set up a series of meetings with key people at one of his hotel-group clients. I joined him.

We met with the food and beverage manager, Brian, who Jack had worked with for years. They shared a warm and friendly relationship.

In the car on the way to the meeting, Jack told me, 'I normally arrive with a box of chocolate croissants but today I've brought a box of choc-chip cookies. Brian loves these and his kids love them even more.'

Food and beverage managers are responsible for buying quality products that meet guest expectations. They know the food industry and want only the best. They are most concerned about the guest experience, then it comes to eats and drinks. The continental breakfasts need to be prepared perfectly and laid out on time every day. The confectionery for high tea, a high-margin product, needs to be special and unique to the hotel's brand.

Brian welcomed us at his office. He and Jack had long dispensed with the formal handshake, which had morphed into a big hug.

'The guest experience is everything in this business,' Brian told us. 'It's influenced by so many things: location, room design, hotel layout, pricing, food ... But a lot of what impacts on the guest experience is not even in our control,' he said with frustration. 'From the experience they have at the airport and at customs, to their shuttle and how much time they spend in traffic, there are a thousand little things that stack up to create the guest's experience. My section is responsible for at least 40% of these. Jack's baked goods and confectionery meet our standards well.'

Jack smiled. As the meeting drew to a close, I asked, 'Who else is responsible for making the purchasing decisions regarding Jack's goods in the group?'

'Oh, yes, of course, let me take you through to Adrian, the finance manager. I have arranged for you to meet him like Jack asked.'

We entered the next office and behind the desk sat a pinched, tight, cold man. He was poring over documents and spreadsheets on the desk before him. We sat and waited.

'I'll be with you in a minute,' he said, not even looking up.

Brian left us.

I saw that the documents Adrian was scrutinising were Jack's product and price lists. Adrian had little interest in Jack's products and range. Food normally warms people up to you, but it had no impact on Adrian. The conversation

Purpose and Positioning

focused only on pricing and delivery costs.

At one point, in order to bring the conversation back around to Jack's favourite topic, his croissants, Jack said, 'Quality products need quality ingredients. Our recipe and ingredients create a croissant that is crispy and flaky on the outside but soft and chewy on the inside.'

He was met with a blank stare. 'I'm sure,' Adrian responded. 'How can you adjust your price to meet my targets?'

That's it: the giveaway is cost targets, I thought. *It's the finance manager's job to want everything for nothing.*

Our meeting ended in half an hour. Again, on leaving, I asked, 'Who else is involved in purchasing these products, Adrian?'

'Oh, yes, Brian said I should send you off to procurement,' he said, explaining to us how to get to procurement manager Thabo's office.

I was dreading this meeting because I knew Jack was likely to go on about his croissants again. We stepped into Thabo's office. It was sterile and minimalist, with a clean, empty desk, a branded writing pad, a sharp pencil and two pens – black and red – in parallel with the writing pad. A trim, upright man sat behind the desk. Thabo was neatly and simply dressed, and he seemed to be immaculately groomed, with his hands folded on his lap.

'Welcome,' he said, peering at us through his round spectacles.

Thabo was risk averse like few other creatures on earth. He quickly asked the inevitable question, one that made perfect sense given he was responsible for health and food safety:

'Could you supply the recipe for your croissants?' Then he fired off two more: 'Could you confirm where you get your ingredients from? How do you know your bakery is free of pests and vermin?'

Jack, a proud man, whose recipe for the perfect croissant was a family heirloom, turned red in the face. Thabo hadn't even been coy in asking for it.

'So, to be clear, Thabo,' I said, 'you need to know these things because you are only concerned about food safety and health?'

Thabo nodded.

'And that is an essential ingredient of the guest experience?' I asked.

Again, he nodded.

'And if you are certain that the ingredients are bought from registered and certified free-trade suppliers and that the occupational safety and health accreditations in Jack's bakery are up to date and registered, that'll put your mind at ease?' I continued, looking at Jack, digging my knee into his.

All the while, Thabo nodded. After a delicate 45-minute meeting, Thabo escorted us to the next office.

This final meeting was the most surprising of all. It was with Lindiwe, the human-resources manager. Her message was simple and clear: she told Jack not to even consider asking to become a supplier if, in doing so, the hotel would have to employ more people or train their current staff to onboard his products. We thanked Lindiwe for her time and that concluded our visit.

Jack had similar meetings with his other hotel-group clients.

They all followed the same process, script, and spoke to the same issues, concerns and requirements. It was a successful month of true insight. Jack, all 55 years of him and with all the experience in the baking industry one would want, was getting an insight on how to, for the first time, market and sell differently into the hotel industry.

It happens to all of us. We all get too close to our businesses to see the wood for the trees. Many of us are guilty of being product-focused without even realising it. While croissants mattered in Jack's business, they were only a part of the whole. There were many more parts that needed to be understood and added together to create a winning customer experience. That is what positioning is all about.

The first building block to creating an Asset of Value, positioning, was finally in place. We understood what problems Jack's hotel-group clients faced in buying freshly baked goods and confectioneries. We also understood who made the decisions and what kept them up at night. We were clear on how their performance as key staff in the hotel-group structure was evaluated and what got them hired or fired. In addition, Jack now also knew what kind of experience his customers wanted when having their problems solved. Now we needed to make sure that Jack gave them this experience all the time.

Positioning leads to purpose

Everything in your business must be built off your understanding of your positioning. The clearer your positioning is, the more certain and confident you will be in leading your business in the direction it needs to go in and the action you need to take.

Weak or poorly articulated positioning will lead to misguided actions, investments, hires and decisions. It fragments and crumbles your businesses platform, leads to a life of chaos and frustrations and will ensure that the business you have built will never be saleable. No amount of hard work, investment or hiring will fix it.

Positioning cannot be built around products, price or service
Like Jack, most business owners believe that their products and services alone make them special and use this to define their positioning. This way of thinking dates back to the mid-1800s when Ralph Waldo Emerson, an essayist, lecturer, philosopher and poet, said, 'Build a better mousetrap and the world will beat a path to your door.'

In the 19th century, Emerson was right. There were hardly any products around. Simply having one meant business! But today, there is too much competition for this to hold true. Those who claim good service makes their business special are similarly misguided.

Some business owners use price to position their business. 'Price is the thing that makes us special,' they claim. This is unconvincing. It is difficult to sustain a price advantage in a competitive market. If you are not in a competitive market, then price probably doesn't matter in any event because it is constantly being driven down.

So many business owners I meet with argue that what makes their business special is superior service. It soon becomes clear that their service is not the result of a good System of Delivery but of the personal attention they or their employees pay to clients. But personal service does not build or make a business. System-driven service is what generates a reliable customer experience. Designing and building this into the business gives you a distinct advantage.

Position your business to treat customers as individuals, not segments

Marketing experts claim that you should position your business based on the particular customer segments you serve. This entails using demographics to identify groups of similar consumers based on age, location, race, gender, education and income, and claiming that your business is special because it targets a particular group. In the business-to-business market, the groups may be segmented by location, turnover, sector and industry.

This way of thinking is terribly outdated. In fact, it is fundamentally lazy and sloppy. Today's world is so fragmented that prescribed definitions of segments are too broad to be of any use in generating a unique position for your business. This is a dead-end strategy. Access to information and increased competition means customers have more choices and buying options than ever before. Rather than treating your customers as segments, treat them as unique individuals requiring tailored customer experiences to suit their needs. Get this right first and then worry about building your business to scale and accelerate.

Welcome to the experience economy. It's here that your positioning should be rooted. Clearly defining your customer and your specialisation is what will set you apart and make you hard to compete with. It's here that customers and clients will talk about you, stick with you and secure your future. This is difficult to get right in the beginning, harder to maintain as you grow, but vital to secure your value. Positioning determines the design of the hull of your ship, and having the wrong hull will see all of your dreams wrecked and mean all your efforts will have been in vain.

Avoid positioning your business around 'solutions'

Some businesses define their positioning by offering what they call 'solutions' to customer segments. These segments are defined so widely and superficially that they are of no use. In using 'solutions' in your positioning statement, you risk not going into the detail necessary to create a powerful positioning statement. This statement should be well defined and deeply considered. It must capture the emotional, physical and cost-saving aspects of the customer experience you provide that will distinguish you from your competitors.

Define customer problems in as much detail as possible

It is important to have a deep understanding of the customer problems you are solving. This is not a simple task and requires translating the problems into emotive, practical solutions for customers. It involves defining your customer as more than a single organisation or individual. Without being

Purpose and Positioning

able to quantify the problems you solve for customers, how can you claim to bring value to them?

At Aurik, we see daily that getting this right is what sets focused, successful business owners apart from others. Five years ago, Carien and I met James and his wife Annie, who were convinced there was a gap in the market but didn't know how to specialise their jewellery display business to take advantage of it. What we learned from working with them was that identifying what your customers really need can help you determine what could make you special and relevant to them. James and Annie managed to find an inventive way to position their business by saying to their customers, 'Your growth problem is ours, too. If we help solve it, our business will grow along with yours.'

James and Annie – Solving your customers' growth problem

The value of asking 'why?' is immense. Asking 'why?' – Why do your customers buy from you? Why do they need you to solve certain business problems for them? Why do customers need you? – can help you lead your business out of stagnancy into growth.

Take a moment to think about whether you are happy with the results of your business. Is the reward worth the effort you put in? If your answer is no, the solution may be found in understanding your relevance. Is your business relevant to your customers, and if so, who are you relevant to, and how relevant are you to them?

Businesses built around products as their defining feature are often only relevant to the product designer or the owner who is in love with the product. It happens easily. A great product produces a propaganda that we begin to believe since it often contains the dreams and aspirations produced by our own egos and image of the world. Often, the positioning of these businesses has little to do with their customers' lives and realities.

Figuring out what is relevant to our customers is not a simple task. The first thing we have to overcome is our fear of speaking and listening to our customers. Many of us don't want to engage with them on a meaningful level because we are scared they will criticise or reject us. Once we have overcome that hurdle, the next thing we need to do is figure out the right questions to ask. Open-ended questions, ones that cannot be answered simply with 'yes' and 'no', are the best to use to encourage full, meaningful answers that will expose the customer's opinions or feelings.

James and Annie had bought their business a few years earlier from James's previous boss who had opted to retire and leave the industry. The business imported jewellery display and packaging products such as jewellery trays, necklace, earring and bracelet displays, gift boxes, drawstring pouches and rotating and locked displays. They supplied these products to local jewellery stores.

James and Annie felt they had a number of advantages in a tired and traditional industry that was broken in many ways. All jewellery display businesses, including their own, imported their products from China, and there was no innovation in the industry. Customers were ready for something new. Their two biggest competitors were owned by business people in their mid-to-late 60s, whereas James and Annie were in their 30s. They had enough experience in the sector to know what would and wouldn't work. Working in a sales role in the business before he and Annie bought it, James had experience in listening to the complaints of customers, having to tolerate his former boss's reluctance to change.

'We know there is an opportunity to take the market and lead it in a new direction,' James began. 'We are just not sure how to do this.'

'How do you know there's an opportunity?' I asked.

'I was in sales for 12 years before we bought this business, Pavlo, and in the last six or seven years, the industry has not grown. Our competitors are getting old and tired and there is no innovation. If we can innovate, we can win, and that's why we bought the business,' he responded.

In his answer, I did not hear the customer's voice. 'What are you going to do to innovate?' I asked.

'Right now, we get 99% of our products from China. We have limited ranges because we need to order big quantities of a limited range to ensure our prices are competitive. It makes for boring displays. We and our competitors all look the same and the battle is being fought on price. Jewellers see us as a reluctant spend knowing that they have to display their products. We are just a cost to them, so they fight us on price all the time. We think that, manufacturing locally, we can create more interesting displays and packaging solutions as well as have a greater variety for our customers.'

James was right. All jewellers looked the same to consumers who drifted past their shop windows. Still, I did not hear the customer's voice in James's answer. I heard the customer complaining about price and the investment needed in what they saw as a grudge spend, but nowhere in James's idea of innovation did the customer's voice come through. The innovation centred on product, and product was perceived to be the problem.

James and Annie agreed to set up a series of meetings with their more familiar customers. Together, we prepared an exhaustive set of questions and role-played how these customer visits would take place. We agreed their purpose was to listen to their customers and learn about their experiences in order to identify opportunities. It was a frustrating exercise, but James and Annie were committed.

'Why do you buy jewellery display units?' James asked David, the first customer he and Annie visited.

'Because I have to display my designs, James, you know that as well as I do!'

'Why do you have to display the designs?' James asked.

'So that potential customers can see what I have to offer.'

'Why do potential customers have to see what you have on offer?'

'So they can buy my jewellery.' David was confounded.

'David, please bear with us,' Annie intervened. 'Why will they buy the jewellery if they can see it?' she asked.

'Because my designs are special and the ranges I have are well put together.'

'What makes them special, David?' Annie asked, looking at the jewellery in the cabinets.

'My designs carry a legacy based on my father's heritage as one of the foremost journeymen in South Africa. We have a history and we have awards. Did you know that my dad was the first journeyman to design a bird made of pure gold and gems? That's the legacy that we are known for and that's the legacy that we carry forward in our jewellery design.'

'If you communicate that legacy effectively, what does it do for customers?'

David could now see where this irritating process was going and with that he answered enthusiastically, 'Annie, design and the idea that the design is unique and carries heritage is what builds confidence in the purchase of jewellery. Think about it. Engagement and wedding rings are some of our best-selling items. Due to political uncertainty, people are buying jewellery less for investment these days. When you buy a gift of jewellery for someone special – for anniversaries, example, and to show love and commitment – the design and the story behind it is what is important, and this is what we offer.'

'How do the displays help with that?' James asked.

'It's not the displays that sell the jewellery, it's the story! The story conjures up the romance and the emotions that get the ring sold,' David replied, and then he added, visibly irritated, 'But I buy displays because I have to. Displays don't sell my jewellery.'

And in that lay the seed to innovating this industry. James and Annie visited three more customers. They were tough interviews, because the customers regarded jewellery display as an obligatory purchase, so James and Annie thanked each customer with gifts accompanied by handwritten thank-you notes.

In asking these questions, James and Annie set themselves up as the new kids on the block in the industry. They took the risk of their customers thinking them to be complete novices. But the interviews allowed the real conversations to begin between James and Annie, and most importantly, for solutions to be found.

Back at the office, James and Annie set about revisiting their product-innovation strategy. First, they recapped what they had learned about the market and articulated the problem being experienced by jewellery retailers. The jewellers were taking strain in the retail end of the business. Located in shopping malls, their ability to draw a customer into the store was dependent on the shop-front window acting as a compelling point of sale. To achieve this, the merchandising and presentation of jewellery were critical. It had to look good and it had to get the passing shoppers into their store. At the same time, the jewellery display options available to the store owner were limited. Consumers walking past the stores all saw the same displays, leaving them uninspired at a time when the economy was making purchases price-sensitive.

The answer lay in offering unique, customised displays to each store. The story of each store, what inspired the designs and choices of the jewellery, needed to be presented as the point of difference between them. Some stores wanted to communicate investment, others romance, some beautiful design, and others confidence in quality.

Next, store owners did not want to pay for displays they would have to reuse. Windows had to be kept fresh, exciting and they had to change frequently – at least once a quarter, suggested one shop owner. The ultimate measure of a good display is how well it draws people into the store. Once that is done, the window has achieved its contribution to sales.

James and Annie set out to solve these problems with a vigour and energy unheard of in the industry. They turned shop windows into blank canvases, seeing themselves as artists with the ability to articulate the stories of stores in a completely new and unique manner. They took ownership of those windows, their challenge to consistently draw customers in.

Next, they turned to technology to help them build and deliver the displays. They bought 3D printers to create the display units. Until recently, access to remarkable machine-learning, artificial-intelligence, internet-of-things and 3D-printing technologies was limited to big businesses. Today, any growing business, driven with an Asset of Value mindset, can build with a big-business mindset. Entrepreneurially driven SMBs can use a strategy of taking many small, technology-driven steps in quick succession to build with big-business capabilities. This strategy is the preserve of SMBs, given their ability to respond to market forces and changes with adaptability and speed.

James and Annie measured each shop-front window and used Computer-Aided Design (CAD) to create displays that were exact in dimensions and easy to install, accommodating a variety of lighting and display choices. Every three months, they would design a new theme for each customer aligned to the story and heritage of that store's brand.

They further installed a small device at each store's entrance to count the number of customers crossing the threshold. They used the data to measure frequency in terms of the time of day, the day of the week, and the day of the month, and analysed this against the themes and stories of each window within the stores. This data, made intelligible, was then used to inform the store owner of the theme's performance and suggest future themes for merchandising

> and shop-window design. Their pricing model now included a small management fee and a performance fee based on the number of customers who entered the store.
>
> James and Annie reinvented their business and the industry in its entirety. They changed the rules of the game so significantly that their traditional competitors would never be able to compete in the same field again. Jewellery-shop owners, mostly journeymen with a passion for jewellery, no longer owned their shop windows. They no longer had to carry the cost of soon-to-be-redundant jewellery displays. Instead, they could focus on their passion: jewellery design and selection. James and Annie turned a project-based business into a monthly and annuity service business. Their role changed from being a supplier to being a partner of their customers. Their positioning message was simple, 'Your growth is our growth,' and the industry responded. Imagine a competitor walking into a store of one of James and Annie's customers and trying to offer the store owner cheaper, better or newer jewellery displays.

People, consumers and businesses only buy things that solve problems. Adopt this view and you will be embracing one of the core attributes you will need as a builder of an Asset of Value. Similar to James and Annie's experience, this is illustrated by Themba's story, which follows. Themba, whose waste-water-pumping business found itself in a depressed sector, discovered a new way to address his customers' problems, using his product as a vehicle to respond to a changing and difficult industry.

Thembalani – A deep understanding of the problem leads to stellar success

Thembalani was a seasoned pump technician. He had a master's degree in Mining Engineering and a pump pedigree most would envy. He had worked for 25 years for some of the world's biggest mining companies, eventually being promoted to Chief Procurement Officer for one of these. In this capacity, he had visited hundreds of pump factories around the world and bought pumps to remove slurry, chemicals and all sorts of noxious waste from mineshafts.

Demoralised by the poor service he received from his suppliers, and believing he could do better, Themba decided to give it a go. MBA in tow, he set off to build his own business. Within the first month, regret set in. How could he have done this? He had given up a job with big prospects. Resigning had been a nightmare. His bosses had pleaded with him to reconsider, saying they had big plans for him. At 48, he was in the prime of his corporate life.

I first met Themba after he had been in business for nearly two years.

'The pump industry in the mines operate on a break-fix model,' Themba told me. 'When a pump stalls, the shaft manager immediately calls the pump guy or whoever the supplier is to fix the pump fast. A broken pump stalls mining operations, which is very costly to the mine in lost revenue. Shaft managers are most concerned about how much ore can be mined from a shaft, and how quickly and safely this can be done.'

Themba went on to explain how suppliers fixed the problem. The pump technician would find out which pump was faltering in the shaft. He would arrive with his team in his pick-up truck with a brand-new pump in tow. It would take the team a few hours to remove the faulty pump and have a new one installed and up and running. Often, lamented Themba, the faulty pump could be fixed with minimal effort and cost, but shaft managers did not care about cost efficiency as much as they did about operational efficiency. Themba's business was focused on providing the same service other pump suppliers did, only he was trying to do it better than his competitors.

'I don't like the plan, Themba,' I began. 'You're simply doing what everyone else does. Why should the market open up for you? There is nothing special about your service and if you do get traction in the market, you'll be trapped in a pricing game and worse, relying on project- and event-based revenues. These are not consistent and make for a horrible valuation at the end of it all.'

We devised a plan of action to find another way of doing things. A way that would set Themba apart in the well-established, highly competitive pump industry. It all began with him going on a road trip. He would visit the mines and meet with all of the people responsible for procuring pumping services. At the time, the mining industry was in turmoil. The mines were stuck in the longest mining strike in South Africa's history. Assets worth billions of rand were being mothballed as the stand-off between mining houses and unions stretched over five months. Furthermore, the mines have no control over global commodity prices and the only thing they can control is costs. Their single-minded obsession is optimising their assets. The timing of Themba's road trip could not have been better, since it is only when problems appear that clients begin to open their eyes and ears to new ideas and solutions.

We met for coffee six weeks later, after Themba had been to visit his customers.

'I'm embarrassed,' Themba said after we ordered our coffees. 'After all my years of being in this industry, after staring at the problem day in and day out during that time, it took this activity you sent me on to see the switch that, if flipped, will build a great business.'

Themba went on to explain the basics of the problem, drawing it for me on a napkin on the table: 'At the beach, if you dig a hole in the sand it will fill with water in a few seconds. If you don't remove this water, the walls around your hole collapse and you are prevented from digging deeper. Whether mines are operating or not, waste water needs to be removed at the risk of the entire mine collapsing in or becoming an underground aquifer.' He was animated.

I smiled, knowing that the insight he was about to share would ignite his drive to build a different business and lead him to forget all he thought he knew, all that crowded out his vision and all that generated the noise, preventing him from hearing what the market wanted, needed and cried out for.

'I'm not in the pump business,' he said. 'I'm in the waste-water-removal business.' He beamed.

He was right. The two are worlds apart. We had devised what we thought would be an answer to waste-water-removal problems faced by the mining houses. The break-fix model was an expensive one. If Themba could provide waste-water-removal systems to the mines, they could remove the cost of pumps and pump maintenance from their balance sheets. Themba could be paid per hectolitre of water pumped.

Themba proceeded to tell me more about the problems his customers were facing and how this was creating pressure everywhere. The environment had changed; mines were getting deeper and more dangerous; conflict between the unions and mines was escalating; the social costs of mining were creeping up; and governmental regulations and licensing were making things almost impossible. The mines were finally ready for change. They are such traditional businesses in every sense of the word, but the pressures they faced had them crying out for answers and it didn't matter where the answers came from or what shape they took. That's the wonderful thing about necessity and desperation: it is the key driver of innovation and change, the elixir of a true-blooded entrepreneur.

Themba went on to write out some calculations on the napkin regarding waste-water-removal and how much the mines would save.

Paper napkins are very useful when meeting with business owners, I thought. I then asked, 'Did you struggle to get the meetings?'

'No. And it wasn't because people remembered me or felt that they owed me anything,' he said with a surprised look. 'The strike and terrible conditions in the mining sector have everyone with their backs against a wall. I simply said I would save them money and that meant I could solve their pump crisis at no cost to them. Boom, the doors opened!'

I was not surprised; problems are precious indeed.

Discarding the business plans he had devised while studying his MBA, Themba set to work building a business that had little to do with pumps and everything to do with cost-effective

Purpose and Positioning

waste-water-removal. Yes, this included pumps, pipes and valves, but its core focus was waste-water-removal. The early stages of an Asset of Value were in the making. This came about by simply orientating the business to being that of a problem-solving rather than a product-pushing one.

A business that responds to the changing environment and that stays close to its customers is a resilient one. This is a business whose owner uses the product or service as the vehicle through which the business can engage with the market. It's such a simple but profound change in attitude and it is 100% in your control.

Themba devised a product that would solve several problems for different people at the same time. The shaft manager would be able to rely on his services; the mine bosses and finance departments could now expect savings from not having to spend money on waste-water-pumping; the procurement department would have less of a headache not having to worry about buying pumps and procuring maintenance services; human resources wouldn't have to hire more pump technicians; and safety would be improved at the mine. The entire solution met the requirements of this complex team of people.

Themba shortly won the right to install his pilot product in one of the shafts at a mine. This included pumps, pipes, valves and everything else that made up his complete waste-water-removal system. He used the pilot project to innovate a new revenue model, one in which, against a service-level agreement, he would be paid per hectolitre of waste-water pumped.

The results were remarkable, and what this new approach sparked was even more exciting. With the pilot having gone well, Themba's next job was to build the systems needed to support his business.

What was particularly interesting was how we managed to create something positive in an industry that was widely reported on in the media as being in disarray. This was a time tens of thousands of people had to suffer through. The impasse was bad. Many suppliers to the mines battled and most closed down. Choosing to adopt a depressing and fateful attitude to the environment was almost a given. It was infectious; bad news followed more bad news. Many people lost their jobs, compounding the strike. It spun the industry into a vicious cycle of collapse.

Yet, the Asset of Value lens through which we looked at the environment led to a completely different approach. Themba succeeded where some of his larger and better-resourced competitors failed. The key to his success was taking the view that problems are precious opportunities to reshape your business in order to make it relevant and resilient. Themba's problem of not being able to gain traction in his well-established market seemed at first to be insurmountable. But using the Asset of Value mindset cracked the problem open to reveal how to turn it into Themba's greatest opportunity. Themba is also a classic example of how necessity drives innovation and innovation should not be undertaken for its own sake. Had his business been doing well, he would never have had to find a different way of doing things in order to succeed.

Clearly defined positioning needs to be backed up by a System of Delivery

The direction of Jack's business was now clear. Beyond the delicious products he made using secret recipes and the best ingredients in town, Jack understood why he existed: to solve

Purpose and Positioning

well-defined problems for his hotel-group clients and create tailored customer experiences for them. The simplicity of this, the idea that Jack could fundamentally change the way hotel groups bought freshly baked goods and confectionery, reignited his energy and drive to the same levels they had been at when he started his business. It was as if a dark, heavy fog had lifted for him and the clarity of his purpose brought his confidence back. Destination set, Jack would now build his business with new purpose. He was a different man to the one I had first met.

I was landing at Heathrow Airport at the start of a busy two weeks in the UK. We had some clients across the UK and the USA who I visited every three months. I switched my phone on before the in-flight announcement invited us to. It beeped with messages for what felt like a full minute while I tried to muffle it, my fellow passengers staring blankly at me, shaking their heads in disapproval while the airhostess arching into the aisle glared at me angrily. I was impatient and had a lot to do. The messages were all from Jack.

I called him the moment I climbed into my Uber ride to my first scheduled meeting.

'I've been trying to get hold of you for ages,' answered Jack. 'I need to see you. Where are you and can we meet in the next half an hour?'

This guy: he really was something. 'Sure,' I said. 'I'm out and about, so why don't we meet at MUD in Mitcham Road in an hour,' I replied, irritated.

'Great, see you then.' He ended the call.

I smiled. I knew Jack would phone in a flash once he googled MUD and saw it was in a continent and country far away from his offices back in Johannesburg. Seconds later, my phone rang. 'I'm in London, Jack, what's so urgent?' I answered.

He was frustrated. Positive and energised, but frustrated. He had certainty of purpose in how he wanted to communicate with the hotel groups, but his team was letting him down. This meant he had to intervene almost every day on almost everything from marketing to sales to operations and procurement.

'You know that story you told me about your time on ships?' he asked. 'Well, that's how I feel right now. I'm constantly running from the engine room to the bridge and back. Just as I want to make the ship go faster, I get called back down into the engine room. I can't get my team to do what needs to be done so we can sail more smoothly.'

'It's not your team, Jack, it's your systems,' I responded. 'I have a plan. I'll be back in a fortnight and we'll get it fixed.'

'A fortnight? Why so long?' He was irked. Jack must be one of the most impatient people I have worked with!

We went back to the drawing board to fix Jack's problem. We needed to ensure his new positioning could be backed up by systems that allowed the business to operate smoothly. Jack could not be the solution on his own. There were not enough hours in the day, and Jack constantly being summoned into the engine room would stall the business's growth.

Purpose and Positioning

The way the business operated needed to be rebuilt to make sure that it could consistently deliver the customer experience required by the hotel groups. It also needed to be able to do this at scale, to meet the growing demands faced by the business as the hotel groups responded to Jack's new positioning. Failure to build these reliable systems would not only constantly pull Jack back down into the engine room but also result in costly leakages and severely harm the business's brand and Jack's reputation.

'Think about it, Jack,' I began when we met again at Aurik's offices. 'We have leaks in the hull pulling you away from the bridge of your ship. If we don't fix them now, the faster you go, the greater the leaks will become.'

Jack had been here many times before and readily agreed.

'We need to build your System of Delivery,' I continued. 'It's a grind in the beginning but worth it in the end if you want to build your business beyond what you have today.'

I looked at him as he thought about it. By getting the business's positioning right, Jack had more than doubled his revenue, to R120m, since we had first met 30 months back.

'I'm already grinding,' he said as he smiled at me. 'Let's do it.'

❏ **Positioning** is about identifying what makes your business truly special – what gives you a distinct advantage over your competitors? – and building it around that. It is the foundation on which your business must be built. Every investment, decision and action must be in service of it in order to

- deepen your speciality in the market. It results in innovation in the short term, annuity cashflow in the medium term and a high business valuation in the long term.
- What makes your business special cannot simply be the products, services or prices you offer. These advantages disappear the moment a competitor offers a better product or service at a cheaper price. True value comes from solving problems for your customers. What needs do they have over and above your products and services?
- In order to identify your customers' greater needs, you should engage deeply with them. By doing so, you will also come to understand the particular experience they will want from you in having their problems solved. It is up to you to ask them the many difficult open-ended questions and to really listen to what they have to say. Your business's future and sustainability depends on you developing this habit and getting it right.
- Once you have defined your positioning, your **purpose** in delivering on your business's promise to your customers will follow. While positioning is what makes you different to your competitors, purpose is what motivates you to do what you do; it generates meaning in your work, which in turn drives your passion and draws people with similar values to your business. This creates an authenticity that makes your business distinct and animates your brand.
- Look closely at your website to understand how you have defined the purpose of your business. Is the content all about you and your products, or is it about your customers

Purpose and Positioning

and the problems you solve for them? Increasingly, people only see and hear what they want to. Your communication will only resonate with potential customers if you have truly understood what problems you solve for them and the customer experience they require.

❏ Only a purposeful captain can lead her or his ship and its crew successfully to its destination. Without a simple, clear purpose, the ship and its crew are doomed to be lost out at sea with insufficient supplies. But every purpose carries a cost. This means you have to know when to say no to your team and your customers. You cannot be everything to everyone.

❏ By always being in touch with the needs of your customers and making sure you respond to changes in their environment, you will be building a resilient business, one that will remain relevant to your customers and give you an advantage in your market.

Chapter 6

Building a System of Delivery

'Should you find yourself in a chronically leaking boat, energy devoted to changing vessels is likely to be more productive than energy devoted to patching leaks.'
– Warren Buffett

Once you have positioned your business well and your purpose is clear, your next step in creating an Asset of Value is to build your System of Delivery. Think of this as the engine that turns your ship's propellers, moving your business forward. There are six main parts to your engine. Each of them has its own purpose, but they need to work together in harmony to produce a consistent, predictable purr as you sail your ship across the open seas.

1. Marketing – the lead-generation engine, measured by how many leads (potential customers) are produced each month;
2. Sales – the conversion engine, measured by how many of the monthly leads are converted into business customers;
3. Operations – the fulfilment and delivery engine, measured

by the consistent delivery of service of a specified quality of customer experience;
4. Procurement – the buying engine, measured by the ability to buy the right things at the right price and the right time to keep the marketing, sales and operations engines running reliably and predictably;
5. People – the most difficult engine to get right but the most valuable and rewarding one, measured by how well you are getting the right people with the right attitude to do the right thing at the right time for the right price; and
6. Money – the engine that manages the supplies to sustain the business and support its accelerated growth.

In an Asset of Value, each part of the engine has to run smoothly to produce consistent forward motion by delivering a reliable customer experience as defined by your business's positioning. A well-built system eliminates friction, breaks down less often, uses less fuel and gets you to your destination faster. It also frees up your time to be on the bridge, from where you can direct and lead your crew and look out for threats and opportunities ahead. Most importantly, a reliable engine supports the big moves you make to accelerate the growth of your business.

As highlighted in the drawing in this section, each of these parts is designed around a number of activities organised into a logical sequence and run by dedicated and capable system operators. Each system operator must be well trained in performing her or his job. Their role must be clearly defined by a job description that specifies what they do and how they are to do it. They must have access to training materials and be rewarded fairly for their work.

Business systems

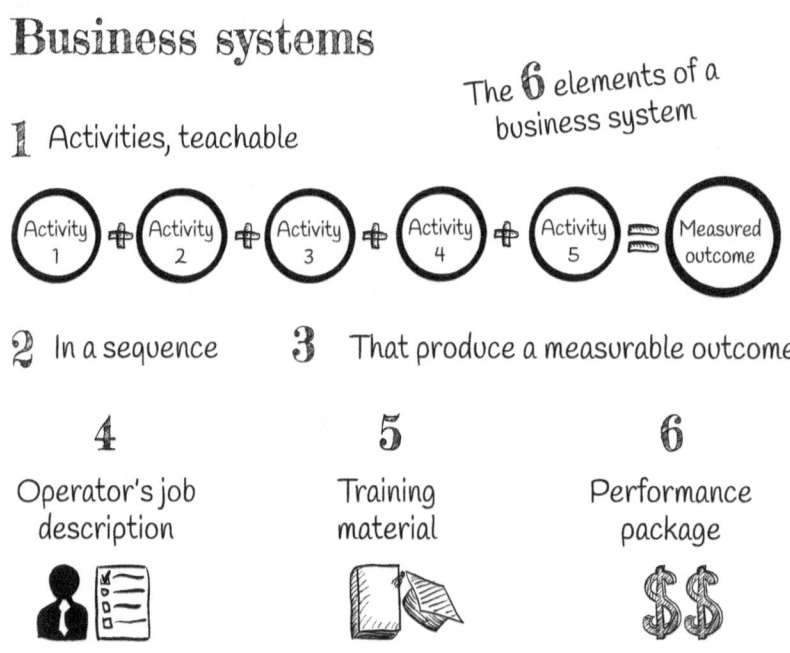

The size of your engine will be determined by your purpose. Who are your customers? What problems do you solve for them? What customised experience do you need to create for them? The answers to these questions will determine the size and kind of crew you need, the size of the cargo load you can carry and the investment you will need to make in fuel and supplies. In a well-built ship, all parts work together to drive the propellers efficiently and consistently.

As the captain, you also need to be able to measure the performance of your ship's System of Delivery. You need access to data, which you can read off your dashboard on the bridge. This will enable you to tweak the design of each part of the engine and to better manage the system operator responsible for its performance.

Everything can be measured in a well-designed System of Delivery. Marketing is measured by the number of leads generated; sales by the number of leads converted; operations by the extent to which the customer's experience is delivered; procurement by the quality and price of products and services purchased; and human resources by the extent to which the right people are doing the right thing at the right time.

Building Jack's first system
The first step Jack took in building his System of Delivery was to create a system in how he marketed to his customers.

'You need to set up a lead-generation system for your marketing,' I told him when we next met.

'What's a lead-generation system, Pavlo? Are you trying to use consultant-speak to sound fancy?' Jack teased me.

There was much banter in our exchanges now. My client was becoming my friend.

'We need to create a system to how you market to your customers, Jack. This needs to be based on what we have defined as the problem we are solving for them. Importantly, by creating a system, we'll be able to measure the results of your marketing and see how many leads it is generating so we can tweak and improve it.'

Jack loved the idea. What business owner wouldn't?

We agreed to stick to email communications because that's what the hotel groups preferred. But now, in addition to sending promotional emails only to the food and beverage managers, Jack would email the finance, procurement and human-resources managers at the 60 hotel groups he targeted.

He would craft each email to resonate emotively and logically with its intended audience, customising the images, structure, language and data to address the key performance indicators against which the recipient was being measured by her or his employer:

- A promotional email to the food and beverage manager would include a picture of a delicious-looking, steaming-hot croissant with a cup of coffee on a table in a beautiful hotel setting. The content spoke to the quality of the ingredients of the croissant and its artisanal French baking process that gave it a crispy outside and a soft, chewy inside. It also spoke to how the guest's experience, first thing in the morning, set the tone for her or his relationship with the hotel.
- A promotional email to the finance manager would include a picture of a piggy bank being squeezed tightly by a thick leather belt. The content spoke to the economies of scale in Jack's procurement and manufacturing processes, his automated efficiencies and his hassle-free delivery system, which enabled him to offer them cost savings on his products. It also highlighted the potential cost savings of the hotels getting rid of their on-site bakeries in favour of

procuring outsourced freshly baked goods.
- A promotional email to the procurement manager would include a photo of Jack's recipe room, better known as a recipe laboratory, in which his bakers wore white from head to toe and worked in a white room, wearing white hairnets and boots. There was not a speck of dirt to be seen in this clinical setting. The content spoke to Jack's insistence on using fair-trade suppliers, quality control, health and safety processes, and adherence to international standards on food safety (even including, for example, particular mention of ISO 22000:2005 on food-safety management systems).
- Finally, a promotional email to the human-resources manager would include a picture of a worker with six arms. The content spoke to the ease of onboarding and storing Jack's products, with no staff training required.

Next, Jack developed a timeline with optimal dates to send his promotional emails. The managers were swamped with reports at month end, so Jack opted for mid-month.

Jack sent his first emails out, and two days later, called the managers he had met with when developing the positioning of his business, confirming if they had received his emails, whether they had read them and what they liked or disliked about them. A week later, he counted the responses he had received and noted which managers these had come from.

With that information on hand, he made a number of small adjustments to the emails for the next month. Most importantly, he had, in his first email drive, the beginnings of measurable results.

Predictably, a week after the first email campaign, Jack phoned me. I was at dinner with some clients who were selling their business to an American buyer looking to establish an African presence.

'Excuse me for a minute, gentlemen,' I apologised, stepping out of the room.

'Hi, Jack, can I call you back tomorrow? I am ...'

'Quickly, guess what the response rate from our first email campaign was?' he interrupted. 'Across the 60 or so hotel groups we market to monthly, I received 556 enquiries from the individual hotels, Pavlo. That's a 202% increase on what we were getting before on the same promotion. Have a good evening.' He put the phone down.

I returned to the table with a broad smile and quietly sat down.

If you want to remain on the bridge of your ship, you will need a dashboard of data

Seeing Jack use the data generated from his marketing system to improve his promotions was thrilling. He tracked the number of leads generated by different combinations of pictures and content in his promotional emails over time. This data formed the basis for Jack's dashboard, which he used from the bridge of his ship.

A ship's dashboard includes all the sophisticated instruments the captain needs to ensure each system in the ship is running well. The captain relies on data to inform her or his decisions regarding navigation, the ship's propulsion and the amount of fuel required to reach the destination.

Carien and I learned the value of data while building our businesses, but helping Jack build his System of Delivery made us realise its significance even more in building an Asset of Value. Before working with clients at Aurik, we agree on certain growth targets, which we use as a basis for being remunerated for our work. Without a plan of action, goals are simply dreams. And in implementing a plan of action that cannot be measured, assessed and tracked against time you run the risk of running out of supplies before you reach your destination.

Each system Jack built could be measured and was built as an indicator into his ship's dashboard. Jack and I celebrated each system indicator coming alive on his dashboard with a series of stiff tall lattes and his chocolate croissants – the best in the world, as I was constantly reminded.

After building his marketing system, Jack moved onto building his sales system. The enquiries resulting from his lead-generation system had to be converted. This is the sole function of sales. Sales do not rely on a broad smile, good looks and a congenial personality. It is a system of storytelling. And a story is made up of activities. These activities, organised into a sequence, contain the elements necessary to convert an enquiry into a customer.

Carefully considered, properly done and consistently

applied, these activities should address how the specific problem the business is solving for the customer will be dealt with. This is only possible if the first building block of an Asset of Value – positioning – is in place, and if the lead-generation system has been properly built. Otherwise, sales will be an arduous, hit-and-miss task.

A good lead-generation system brings to your door what I refer to as 'on-point leads', which are enquiries from customers you identified as being central to your business's positioning. The right lead will respond to a well-structured lead-conversion process, resulting in a sale.

After building his sales system, Jack would focus on building a system for his operations. This system needs to be flawlessly designed. Once a customer agrees to buy your product or service, the messaging they received from your lead-generation and lead-conversion systems will create an expectation of the experience they will have, which your operational system will need to fulfil.

Beware of white knights and silver bullets

Jack took almost two years to develop and bed down his System of Delivery. He had to do this in the midst of running and growing his business every day. It was a 'build-while-you-fly' exercise.

This was in the early years before Carien and I had developed an efficient, structured and organised method to building a System of Delivery, which today we deliver to our clients in nine months.

Building a System of Delivery

I remember vividly the anxiety Jack seemed to experience during this period. It seemed to come without warning in our monthly review sessions.

Concerned for his wellbeing, when I next saw him grimace I asked, 'What was that for?'

'What?' He looked at me quizzically.

'That frown and grunt. Are you in pain?'

'Oh that, yes, well no, not in physical pain. I'm furious that the ERP [Enterprise Resource Planning] system we bought has cost us four small fortunes: one to buy it, one to install it, one to have training in how to use it, and lastly, one to get rid of it and start all over again.'

An ERP system is software that promises to create a System of Delivery by prescribing all your operating procedures, automating some of your back-office functions and generating real-time data. It attempts to integrate, through technology, into a single database and user interface all the functions of the business, from marketing to sales to operations and procurement, and finance and human resources. An ERP system promises to be a System of Delivery in a box, readymade, easily installed and simply operated. It is manna from heaven; an easy way out. Pricy, but easy. I immediately understood Jack's grimace – and this was a special type of grimace – I was to experience it directly myself and would see it on the faces of many other business owners after that day.

A business is complex. There are so many moving parts and as a business grows, so too does its complexity. Small mistakes in a small business are survivable. Small leaks in the hull of a small ship are fixable. They're not ideal but you can still sail safely as long as your hull is mostly intact. As a small business grows, those small leaks, left unattended, grow too. They take the shape of unmanaged and escalating costs, incapable and undirected people and many other issues that stack up, building remarkable levels of stress. If not managed, stress wears you down. It drains your energy, making you feel vulnerable; it eats away at your confidence, making you doubt yourself and reducing your passion in what you are doing.

In this state, you are more susceptible to what I call 'white knights and silver bullets'. A 'white knight' is a person who promises to rush to your aid with an immediate solution to your problems. It can come in the form of a new hire, armed with a CV that says your new employee can solve all the problems and challenges your business faces today. A silver bullet is a seemingly simple solution to a complex problem. This can come in the form of an ERP system that promises to give you the structure you need to build and manage your business. An ERP system is not a System of Delivery and there is no short cut to building one, brick upon brick.

Jack had extensively researched the ERP software. He looked at the features, benefits, price and simplicity of use. He wanted an easy solution to a task that seemed formidable.

Jack continued: 'After great expense and effort, Pavlo – you know, with most software, they always make you think it's easy and affordable to install – we eventually got it loaded and programmed our business to fit with it. That's where things first went wrong. I had a vision behind how it should work.

Building a System of Delivery

I knew what I wanted and all the people I had conversations with about it suggested it could do exactly what I wanted and how I wanted it done.'

At that stage, Jack thought he had a clear understanding of his business and clarity on where all the problems lay.

'What went wrong?' I responded.

'Firstly, it wasn't so simple. Secondly, I had to make a number of changes in my business to make the implementation of the software affordable.'

I have seen this so many times before. You buy a piece of 'customisable' software because you want it to fit your business and the way it currently works. Although an ERP system is customisable, you need to contract technical partners to make it happen. 'Affordable' becomes 'insanely expensive' and allocated budgets increase beyond belief. To then manage the cost back down, we let the software determine and guide our systems and in doing so remove all the specific positioning we have developed for the business.

In using an off-the-shelf ERP software you risk your business delivering exactly the same customer experience that other businesses using the same software offer, reducing you to compete on price or service. ERP systems promise that you can adjust and tweak them to differentiate your business and align it with your purpose, but the reality is that this is a costly and time-consuming exercise that doesn't always work.

'It's clear to me now that we didn't even understand our business properly and the problems I hoped the software would solve remain in play. In fact, the software itself has become a problem, making us unresponsive and increasing training costs,' Jack vented.

I agreed with Jack: understand first, automate next, not the other way around.

The greatest hurdle to overcoming an obstacle is taking the first step

'Pavlo, the marketing system is working but I'm stuck on the sales system,' Jack began at our next session. 'It's so people and personality driven that turning it into a system or engine feels impossible.'

Jack was mostly right. It always feels impossible until you start. The idea that sales are only personality driven cannot be accommodated in an Asset of Value. And how you choose to define it is a choice. Relying only on employing charismatic salespeople might work for you in the short term but will fail you thereafter.

'Who has been your best salesperson to date, Jack?' I asked.

'Besides myself?' He smiled. 'We had a lady named Andrea. She was awesome and customers loved her.'

'*Had*?' I tested.

'Yes, Andrea left us about four years ago,' he said bitterly. 'She said she found a better job and upped and left.'

'Where did that leave you?'

'Oh, I was mad. I had made so many accommodations for her because she was good. We paid her well and I never fussed about clock-watching because she produced results and she really innovated our business,' he said, softening as he reflected.

Building a System of Delivery

'What happened to the customers she was responsible for after she left?' I stuck to my line of questioning because I wanted to make a very deliberate point.

'I had to climb in, Pavlo. A number of them threatened to leave because they said she had made promises to them that we weren't delivering on. Some left with her when she went to work for a competitor. It was a real mess and it took some painful work to stabilise the ship again.'

'And innovation? What did she innovate?' I was getting closer to the nub of the issue I wanted to share with Jack.

'She would come in and tell me what customers said they wanted. For example, some of the products we bake were motivated by her. In fact, the entire business of selling flour to small bakeries was a result of her speaking to these customers on sales visits, finding out what they needed.'

I could see Jack was angry with Andrea, but he seemed to miss her too. We paused for a minute. I wanted the emotion to rise up and I wanted the memory of Andrea to come into the present moment. I recalled that the flour-selling part of Jack's business had been the single-biggest drain on Jack's profits and energy, a shocking investment and a massive driver of complexity.

'And who was your worst sales hire?' I asked after a minute or so.

'We had a fellow by the name of André who I fired about six years ago. He was a real b***s****er. This guy had a silver tongue and was so charming. I remember, when I interviewed him, he said all the right things. He had the baking lingo, knew about my business and I seriously had big expectations of him.'

'What happened?' I prodded.

'He was all talk, Pavlo. He constantly promised me deals were in the pipeline. He led me on so badly that I'm embarrassed to tell you about him. This guy always had an answer to everything and anything. I was such a fool to believe him, but at the time we needed sales and I held onto the positive of everything he said. Optimism can skew your sense of judgement badly.'

Jack's anger was returning. I could see him calculating the cost of André in his mind.

To make it worse, I asked, 'How long was he with you and how did you manage him?'

'Almost a year.' Jack looked embarrassed. He felt duped and stupid at the same time. 'Every week, at our sales meeting, I would ask about current and future sales, and he would lie about how much business he was doing. It was hard to manage, you know. His list of customers would grow from one week to the next and the promise of business was hard to ascertain.'

I had prepared for this meeting. Building the sales system is hard to get right. It needs so many iterations and so much fine tuning to be simple and effective. It can be very frustrating but getting it mostly right offers deep, enduring rewards.

Sales is more about a system than a salesperson
'Check this out, Jack,' I said, pointing to some numbers I had

Building a System of Delivery

put together of Jack's business performance over time. These were the same numbers I had used to show Jack the sine-wave pattern his business was generating before he had defined his business's positioning. On them I had marked the start and end dates of Andrea and André's time in the business.

'Both Andrea and André kept pulling you back into the day-to-day sales activities of your business,' I continued. 'You weren't growing over those periods, Jack, and I bet you were still responsible for bringing in the biggest chunk of revenue each month!'

He identified three times when he had brought in big customers who were the most likely cause of growth; three customers he still served. He also saw a slight dip in sales in the period after Andrea's exit, when the everyday orders took time to recoup. He grunted at the evidence of André's tenure in the business revealing little sales.

'So, we have a choice. Do we hope and pray that we find remarkable salespeople, all the time, to accelerate our revenues? Or do we build a sales engine, one that runs consistently irrespective of the sales team's personalities?'

Jack looked at me vexingly.

'Sales is a science more than an art, Jack,' I continued. 'You have reshaped your business to solve a customer problem. The quality of your products matter, but that's not what makes a sale happen. In order to build the sales system, we must start by understanding which customer we are selling to and then design the engagement to resonate with them. They need to feel heard to build their trust in us. They need to feel understood to build their confidence in us. You developed a tremendous amount of insight into the personalities of the key people involved in purchasing your products when you met with the hotel groups; let's try to use that information to tailor sales to each of them,' I offered.

'Let's do it!' Jack's enthusiasm sprung to life again. 'I'm not repeating the same mistakes; not this time. I love the idea of building a sales engine. If we can get it to work, it'll revolutionise my business and free up my time.'

We set up a series of sessions at Aurik to grind through the process. I was really looking forward to it. Inasmuch as Jack's business was going to benefit, all the difficult lessons Carien and I had learned through starting and growing our own businesses was being put into practice with a business in which the marketing system had started producing results.

Similar to how Jack had tailored each of his promotional emails to the food and beverage, finance, procurement and human-resources managers, he now had to customise the sales engagement for each of them. Getting this right required a deep understanding of their experiences and personalities.

The first step to creating Jack's sales system was analysing what motivated his customers. Their reasons for being attracted to work in the hospitality sector rather than, for example, the mining sector, revealed something about how we should sell to them. Whereas mining attracts people who relish technical challenges and like to build things and move earth, the hospitality sector is about people, guest experiences and personal service; it attracts people who like to create a great customer experience and see that reflected on a guest's face. Jack's customers strove to create this value for their guests. We also needed to acknowledge that each hotel group was different and had its own texture, personality and dynamics.

Next, we characterised each of the four types of hotel-group managers that Jack's salespeople would sell to. Each department attracted likeminded people to it. Finance managers, for example, would find meaning and value in their work for different reasons and in different ways to food and beverage managers. Similarly, their job performance was measured differently. What would make each type of manager successful each month? Was it an ingenious cost saving, for example, or a wonderful guest review? As people, these managers also wanted to do well and feel valued. They wanted to progress in their careers and win promotions. How could our sales engagement help them achieve this? Interpreting these dynamics technically and emotively is vital in building the sales system. It goes to the heart of the experience you are creating in solving customer problems.

Building a simple sales system – and it needs to be simple – is not possible without first immersing yourself in this complexity. At first this process is filled with darkness but every time you deepen, refine and redo it, more light begins to appear. The more effort you put into it, the more engagement you have with your customers, the more the light shines and removes the darkness. Over time, the simple clarity of what messaging and behaviour resonates most deeply with your customers emerges. You'll know it when you are there. You'll look back over the work you've done and the distance you've covered and wonder why you made it so complicated in the beginning.

Once you understand your customers deeply in this way, you can build a sequence of activities into a sales system that can be measured and taught.

If purpose is your rudder, your System of Delivery is your engine

Consistently delivering on what your business promises is how you will build your business's brand. This takes time to develop and vigilance to maintain. Your System of Delivery is the engine that generates this consistency. Without this golden thread, you will constantly be pulled back into the engine room.

Jack himself led the development of the sales-system activities. This included creating scripts for the salespeople to use in speaking to customers, brochures and email templates. He organised the sales activities into a sequence that unfolded the value proposition his business offered not only to the hotel group, but also to the individuals in the different departments. Jack himself went to visit his customers. He tested the language and adjusted the emphasis on value as perceived by each of the managers he was selling to.

'Pavlo, it has taken a lot longer than I thought it would,' he said, sitting down for our breakfast session, 'but I have the numbers.' He pushed a piece of paper in front of me. 'Our marketing system generates between 397 to 714 leads a month,

Building A System Of Delivery

depending on the season. Before, we were converting 35% of them. The sales system I built now converts upwards of 46%. That's 31% more than I did before!' He beamed with pride.

It was a big number. But it made sense. When the sales process aligns to the marketing message and promise, the sales engagement equals your customer's expectation. Over time, a consistent customer experience begins defining a customer's view of your business and seeding the trust and confidence it takes to commit to a sale.

'That's awesome, Jack. What's next?'

'Well, I guess it's going to be to build the operations system – for procurement and production – right?'

'Right,' I replied. We were on track.

Carien and I made many such mistakes as Jack did, for example, in purchasing an ERP system, while building the first few of our own businesses. The painful cost of those mistakes profoundly informs the approach we take to building an Asset of Value today. Start with your purpose, then build the System of Delivery to fulfil it consistently. Once you are in control and have a deep understanding your business, find the software that you need to support and enable, not lead and determine, your System of Delivery and team. This is key to preserving what makes your business special.

❏ A **System of Delivery** is the engine of your ship. That engine is made up of different parts, each with an individual system of its own: marketing, sales, operations, procurement, people and money. These systems work together to ensure that

the business runs smoothly.
- ❏ Each system comprises a number of activities. These activities are organised into a logical sequence that addresses the specific problem you are solving for your customer.
- ❏ Each system generates data that you can use to monitor and improve its performance.
- ❏ There is no short cut to building a good System of Delivery. Beware of off-the-shelf software packages that pose as a System of Delivery in a box. These amount to little more than difficult-to-customise 'solutions' that you have to build your business around in order to get them to work. In using them you also run the risk of delivering the same customer experience as your competitors, who are using similar software.
- ❏ Although it is difficult to do, it is possible to build people-centric parts of the business such as sales and human resources into systems.
- ❏ Your System of Delivery's job is to ensure that everything runs smoothly, reliably and predictably so that you can spend more time on the bridge of your ship, from where you can lead and accelerate your business.
- ❏ A good business design with a well-conceived System of Delivery will ensure your business delivers a consistent experience to your customers, which in turn will bring constant business.

Chapter 7

Your Team

'If you want to go fast, go alone. If you want to go far, go together.' — African proverb

Preparing for my fortnightly breakfast meeting with Jack, I had concerns. The business's growth was once again stalling and Jack's time was spent racing up and down the stairs from the bridge of his ship to the engine room and back again. I needed Jack to focus on growth. He wanted to focus on growth.

We went to the coffee shop down the road and stood in line, talking, until we were at the counter.

'Can I help you, sir?' the barista asked.

But before we could place our orders, Jack turned to me and asked, 'What is wrong with people, Pavlo? I mean, why can't they do what they are supposed to? I have taken so much risk in my life to build a business, from the ground up, and through that I have created sorely needed jobs. Yet, it's as if my staff don't respect the jobs they have, and they keep messing up. Honestly, I'm frustrated beyond hell. People don't care. It's as if when you want something done properly, you have to do it yourself!'

'Can I help you, sir?' the barista asked again. The queue was growing, Jack was in his head and the barista – well, he just wanted to make us our coffees and get to the other side of the breakfast rush.

'Two tall lattes, please. Sorry about that,' I said.

After getting our coffees, we went to find a table.

'You have two options, Jack. One: don't grow the business. Two: solve the people problem and grow the business. Which one will it be?' I asked.

'Screw you,' he said, smiling faintly.

I knew that Jack had little choice since he had redefined his positioning, which in turn rebooted him and his inspiration and energy. Yes, he was complaining about the perennial people problem but, when on a mission, this is not a problem; it's simply a challenge. It's not insurmountable; it's simply fixed, and the frustration only comes from how long it takes.

Challenges slow your progress down, and thank heavens for that: it is through dealing with these challenges that the System of Delivery is built more solidly. Solving your human-resources needs in building an Asset of Value means having the right people doing the right thing at the right time and at the right price … every time. There is a rhythm to it, deliberately so. That rhythm, predictable and consistent, allows for predictable and consistent business performance and customer experiences. That, and not big marketing budgets, is what builds a brand.

'Before we solve this, Jack, we need to figure out the "why" and the "how" of the people in your business,' I continued. 'We need to define why they do their jobs and how they do them.'

'What do you mean the "why" and the "how"?' Jack asked. 'The "why" is that I offer people jobs. I created employment for them. The "how" is do your job!' he retorted.

'Let's take stock of where we are,' I said, ignoring his irritation. 'Today you have a problem-solving and customer-experience focused business, using baked goods as a commodity to trade. Your business's speciality is no longer based on the recipes you use.'

Jack twitched and stared at me blankly in reply. While I knew he agreed and fully comprehended what that meant, he still got irked every time I dismissed the value of his family recipes.

'What makes your business special is that you solve specific problems for your customers, from the food and beverage to the finance managers, by delivering the same customer experience ...'

'Yes, of course, I agree with that but what's that got to do with people?' Jack interrupted.

'People follow systems, Jack. We are business builders, and we build systems before we hire people to operate them, and not the other way around. It's your business and you need to be in control, so you start by defining the business, as we have already done, and then you seek to get the business running smoothly, consistently. This needs two things: a System of Delivery and people to operate it.'

A light switched on in Jack's head. His eyes glimmered and he smiled. 'F***, people follow systems ...' he muttered.

Jack set about reconfiguring his entire staffing structure at a senior-management level. It was becoming a big business. He had secured a growing share of the hotel sector and the annual turnover was approaching R328m. Jack needed system operators that would not only run his System of Delivery but also constantly improve it. We began doing a lot of work on sourcing technology solutions to increase efficiencies and certainty in each of the business systems. The system operators led these interventions while managing capacity in their respective systems.

System operators rather than job positions

In the Asset of Value method to building a business, we create systems first and then hire people to operate them. That way, we stand a greater chance of finding the right person to do the right thing at the right time and at the right price. This approach to people is worlds apart from the traditional view of hiring people first and then expecting them to fix the problems of our businesses. As opposed to hiring, for example, a 'marketing manager', we should hire a 'marketing-system operator' when building an Asset of Value.

Reflect on your experience: how many times have you hired a sales or operations person only to be disappointed with the result down the line? I have little doubt that if they were decent people they tried their best. But more often than not, the failure of staff to perform in a business is more our fault as the business owner than theirs as employees.

The conditions that govern how people are traditionally

recruited into a business set both the business owner and the new recruit up for failure. You cannot hope to succeed by copying and pasting your job descriptions off the internet and comparing them against the bullet points of candidates' CVs. Often, the recruitment process is driven by urgency and desperation for a quick-fix solution to existing and growing gaps in the business.

This generates a confirmation bias in terms of which the business owner and team responsible for recruiting will only hear and see what they need to in order to solve the problem. They will also only hear and see what they need to in order to serve their own interests. It's human nature. All of this leads to business owners such as Jack adopting the attitude that it is impossible to hire good people and that they might as well do everything themselves.

Changing your mindset can alter your experience of the people you employ. Instead of using conventional words such as 'manager' or 'head', adopt the term 'system operator' and translate job descriptions into opportunities for your system operators. This will create a new direction for you in terms of how you build your business and employ your staff. Building systems first and employing people to operate those systems next is the most profitable and certain route to ensuring a steady, consistent seafaring journey towards your destination.

Purposeful people power your purpose

People are the single-most valuable resource you can ever have in your business. Even in businesses in which the opportunity for automation is high, people are still needed. Successful automation depends on people. When things go wrong with automation, it is because someone hasn't done something correctly or has neglected a step in the process.

Business is all about people; thank heavens for that. It is also people who bring community and relationships – a culture, a soul – to the workplace. People, too, are the most unpredictable part of your System of Delivery. They have family, personal, work and other issues. They have good days and bad ones. Some care, others don't. Some steal, others are honest.

It is essential to build systems to enable your staff to share your purpose in delivering your defined customer experience because people come and go, while systems remain in place. They give your business structure. Looking at your business in this way allows you to see clearly how to build your business in an organised way rather than as a complex mess of activities and people.

Often, we hire people in the hope that they will be self-starters who need little help in establishing themselves. One such business owner was Oren, an astute and innovative businessman who left his sales staff in his data-services business to try to figure out how to sell a new product without sufficient training or a sales system in place. Oren hired and fired four sales heads in three years until he realised that it wasn't the people he hired who were the problem – it was his lack of a System of Delivery to enable them to do their jobs effectively and with purpose.

Oren – How to delegate effectively

Oren was tall, lean, energetic and smart. After years of working in the telecommunications industry for MTN, Vodacom and Cell C, he started his own data-services business. He serviced the business sector, providing messaging applications for his clients. He had a natural affinity for technology and had high hopes for what the cellular networks could do for South African businesses.

After a formal meet-and-greet session, we got straight to it.

'What led to you starting your business, Oren?' I asked.

'My last few years have seen me jump from one company to another. I did this, Pavlo, because I wanted to lead the development of data services in these companies. Voice revenues will decrease as access to mobile phones and competition among service providers increases. In fact, in some countries, cellular networks provide voice at no cost just so they can hold onto their customers.'

'I'm guessing that the South African service providers weren't interested?' I replied.

'Exactly!' he almost shouted, pacing up and down the boardroom. I felt like I was watching a centre-court match from a front-row seat at Wimbledon.

'They don't get it,' Oren continued. 'They are meant to be innovative businesses and yet they are addicted to voice revenues, which only have a few years left. Data will be the new thing.'

'Innovation is seldom voluntary,' I said. 'Mostly, it is driven by necessity. Why should the service providers innovate if there is no necessity?'

Finally, Oren sat down, deflated. Our discussion turned to Oren's biggest obstacle to sustained growth: people. Many of the business owners we work with at Aurik point to people as being their greatest opportunity and hindrance. As their businesses grow and stretch into new markets and territories, the 'people problem' worsens, creating doubt about future ambitions. They look for quick-fix solutions to this problem, which creates even more complications further down the line.

Over the last three years, Oren had hired and fired four sales heads.

'They all looked so good on paper, Pavlo,' Oren said. 'Here I am, killing myself to keep up with the demand for our services, we're growing at a phenomenal rate, and my sales heads are letting me down. I knew most of them from my time working for the cellular networks, they knew me and understood my vision, and yet, when I signed them, they failed me big time.'

There is little more that irks me than blame. A winning mindset never blames; instead it seeks to understand, adapt, act and permanently solve.

We ended the meeting with me promising to help Oren. I thought he was a good investment in human capital and that he was onto a great idea. I got Oren's permission to contact his former sales heads, three of whom agreed to meet with me while the latest one was still too angry and resentful to do so, having been fired recently.

In the coming days, I met each former sales head individually. I found them all to be experienced, smart and professional.

The problem soon became clear. They had all been excited about

Oren and his vision. As ambitious people, they all saw data as the next big thing. They all wanted to get ahead in the industry and had made big sacrifices to join him. But soon after each of them started, they found themselves isolated on board Oren's newly built ship. The ship was designed differently to the large ones they had sailed while at the big cellular networks. Oren had not built an engine, a System of Delivery, for his ship. He failed to provide his sales heads with a manual and training, so they could not learn how to perform their jobs in order to sail the vessel.

Any good salesperson first needs to learn about a product or service before they can sell it. They need to understand what it is, how it works, why it works and what benefits it offers. Then they need to know who the market is who would find value in the product or service. Once they understand who the market is, they can begin to prospect and make deals.

However, if the product or service being offered is completely new in the market, as was Oren's data-service offering, you need to first do business development – to educate the market on what your product or service does and how it will benefit them. In these instances, the sales cycle will take longer than that for well-recognised products or services in more mature markets. While Oren's sales heads were good at selling products, they were not necessarily good at business development. All of this stayed in Oren's head, unavailable to his salespeople, and his sales heads shortly failed to meet Oren's expectations and were fired.

Two weeks later, Oren and I met again.

I found him pacing in the boardroom.

I took a seat. 'What a great bunch of people,' I began.

He looked at me but didn't respond.

'Tell me about how you employed and managed each of them.'

Oren began talking about each of his former sales heads: where he had met them, why he had chosen them and what he had paid them. Each had her or his own story; each had come on board with a completely different proposition from Oren. The only thing in common was that each sales head was managed in exactly the same way. Oren managed by expectation alone.

'Pavlo, they were smart people and ...'

'*Are*,' I interjected.

'Okay, they *are* smart people, and they should've been able to get the job done. I have no time to babysit senior people and I relied on their experience and understanding of the sector as well as the incentives I put in place.'

I asked Oren to take a seat and then shared what I had learned with him.

'They all admire you, Oren,' I said. 'They all joined you because they were seduced by your energy and vison. They love your enthusiasm, guts and drive. They joined you because they wanted to be part of your vision, and all of them gave up senior jobs to join you. Two were even so excited to work with you that they took a dip in salary. All three told me that upon being hired, you vanished. You were barely around. They were frustrated that there was no handover. Each of them had experience in the provision of voice services and not in the new field of data services, just like everyone else in the sector.'

'But they promised they could do it,' Oren scowled. 'They said so in their interviews and on their CVs. I'm able to do the job they weren't able to, and look, it's working. I'll say it again: if you want something done properly, do it yourself!'

I was reminded of Jack in that instant.

I continued: 'What they really needed was material to work off, Oren. They needed guidance; they needed a "starter kit". If you had provided this for them, all three were confident that they could have gotten off the ground.'

Delegation, when it is done correctly, and when there are proper systems in place first to enable your staff to do their jobs properly, can give you and your employees the confidence you need to perform optimally. A ship's crew determines whether it arrives safely at port or sinks in the middle of the ocean. Every crew member's job is defined within a system of activities, has a well-defined job description specifying their activities and generates a measurable outcome. Crew should be frequently trained to operate the systems, and the captain must regularly manage the standard of their performance. If everyone knows what he or she is supposed to do and how to do it, they will work towards the common goal of getting the ship to your intended destination. It is your responsibility to ensure this.

Where there are skills shortages, the design of the business needs to be adapted. There is no value in bemoaning the fact that you cannot find skilled or credible staff for your business. Just as every ship sails in the same ocean, everyone else in your sector and industry is suffering from the same challenge as you. The smart captain recognises this and adapts the design of the ship or alters its course to accommodate these constraints. The inflexible and foolish captain complains endlessly, unaware that her or his attitude perpetuates a

> psychology of failure.
>
> The smart captain also realises that, even under pressure, your crew might forget the specific things you have said or done in the past, but they will never forget how you made them feel. Oren's lack of guidance left his sales heads feeling bitter and resentful. Your true power as a captain is to always make it easy for your crew to follow your leadership.

As employees, we need to earn our right to work

I recently addressed an audience of about 200 people at a business event in Detroit, sharing my insights into what makes for a winning business mindset.

I told the audience that business owners invest a lot and sacrifice much to create a business that generates employment, often without the support of governments, who pass stringent labour laws and fail to support businesses with enabling economic policies, funding and incentives.

'Private business owners are the true heroes of any society,' I said. 'And often, employees of private businesses also fail to fully realise the value that business owners provide in creating opportunities for them.'

I could see a few audience members sitting up straighter in their chairs. Some appeared to be somewhat ruffled by what I was saying, but I persisted: 'A job is a privilege, not a right, and an employee ought to become the best they can be, independently of the employer, to survive and thrive in their job and beyond it. All employees should be investing independently in their development and education. Doing so will assure them of a job, improved opportunities and dignity.'

Then I said, driving the point home, 'Employees have a responsibility to make themselves valuable to the business. As employees, we need to earn our right to work.'

At this, someone in the crowd shouted, 'B***s***!'

I paused, scanning the crowd.

A man stood up and said, 'You have caused me great offence. How can you say that we have to earn our right to work? My grandfather worked for Ford Motor Company all his life. My father followed in his footsteps and I followed him. Our family has given three generations of service to Ford and I was let go five years back. How is that fair? How have we not earned our right to work?'

A few people in the audience grumbled in agreement.

The man, encouraged by the crowd, went on to introduce himself as Jim, and explained that his family had lived in Detroit for more than five generations. They had their home, their church, their community and had built their identity there. Jim had been unemployed for five years since losing his job at Ford and said it had been impossible to get permanent work. He had flipped burgers and been a janitor from time to time. He had been a production-line supervisor at Ford before losing his job. As things stood, Jim was struggling to put food on the table and had looked at entrepreneurship as a means to create a life for himself.

That, too, is oversold in the USA as a solution to unemployment as much as it is here in South Africa, I thought. I have enormous empathy for any person who is willing to work but who can't find employment. It must be soul destroying.

On the spot, I had to respond: 'Earning your right to work means keeping yourself relevant to employers. That means upskilling yourself all the time. Surely that's a fair trade. As a business owner, if I'm clear on what I need from my team, I employ against that criteria. If I demonstrate that I, as the business owner, meet the very criteria I have set for my employees, I have earned my right to work.'

Jim responded, 'Then the businesses in Detroit have failed us. They are not growing. They are relocating to the West Coast and I cannot afford to move there. We live as a family with my father in his house, the same one my grandfather lived in.'

Again, the audience's sympathy was palpable.

Jim continued, 'Where am I meant to upskill and get my education, as you put it? We have no money.'

I paused and thought about my response. More members folded their arms and the rising anger and tension was palpable.

'Let me tell you a story, Jim. A personal story,' I began in reply. 'Every three years at Aurik, we start a new business. We do this to stay real and close to the coalface of what it takes to start, build and grow in an ever-changing environment. The way we start businesses today is fundamentally different to the way did it three, nine or 15 years ago. The most recent business we started is an app for the retail sector. It needs a lot of software development before it can be brought to market.'

Jim was unmoved. He sat with his arms folded, glaring at me.

'A few months ago,' I continued, 'I was increasingly frustrated by our technical partners, who were doing the programming to develop the app. They were lagging and making excuses all around. That weekend, I met a friend for a coffee, and while waiting for him to arrive I stepped into a bookstore to flip through a few magazines. I passed through the children's section, and there I picked up a book that caught my eye. It was bright and full of drawings. Produced for 12-year-olds, it was a book on learning the Python programming language, the same language my technical partners were using to build the app.'

Jim unfolded his arms and leaned forward slightly.

'A month later, using the book and two free YouTube tutorials, I started to teach myself how to programme in Python. When you learn any programming language, the first thing you usually learn to do is to use code to output the words "Hello World" to the screen. Even though I was terrified that I had no aptitude for the task and would fail, I managed to do this. That first step, just to start, was the most difficult one to take.

'Six months later, Jim, with many distractions, I had created a functioning cryptocurrency I called PavCash. I felt like a genius. I felt like I was the future and all the promises it held. I didn't tell anybody about it, though, because although it worked, I knew that the programming was terrible, complicated and full of bugs. I wanted to avoid being teased and jeered at by my technical partners.'

At this, Jim and a few of the other audience members grinned.

'But what did change, Jim, was that my technical partners

noticed a difference in how I engaged with them. I understood their language and logic and was increasingly drawn into the development discussions. Not that I could help them with the technical side of things, but now I knew what was going on and what the challenges were. What is most interesting is that they now call me from time to time to discuss their business problems. It created a kind of connection between us, much like it does if you speak to someone using their own language.'

Jim grasped the idea. A glint of opportunity appeared in his eyes as he gently nodded.

'If I can, you can, I promise you that,' I said. 'The amount of free resources out there is astonishing and we all, business owners and employees alike, have a responsibility to each other to commit to lifelong learning. To value each other, we must respect each other. To respect each other, we must serve each other. Granted, unemployment in South Africa is systemic to how the economy originated and then was built dating back to the late 1700s. But unemployment is also a choice inasmuch as it is the result of history, here and in the USA. Creating jobs to employ people and reduce unemployment is not a business owner's responsibility alone. Investing in yourself to make yourself employable is your responsibility. If you fail to do this, the next person in line will take your opportunity. Only you can turn "No Job" into "Hello Job".'

I still keep in touch with Jim today. Acting on this idea has given Jim his independence and confidence back. He always replies late to my emails with the same greeting: 'Pavlo, apologies for the late reply – I've been insanely busy.'

Learn to do a job well yourself first before you design systems or hire for it

Jim's dilemma and frustration made me remember with fondness my Building Science university professor, one of the most influential men in my life.

The professor had a big reputation in the civil-engineering and construction sectors, and he had conceptualised the Building Science degree, effectively a blend of civil engineering, quantity surveying and architecture.

I was accepted into the third-ever intake for the degree and studied hard during my first year. After we had written our end-of-year exams, the professor called all 98 of us first-year students into the hall. We were all nervous.

The professor had a reputation to keep, which he had constantly reminded us of in class every week during the first year. 'This degree will be my legacy after retirement,' he always said.

To this end, he would not tolerate anything less than marks well above a simple pass.

'Right, all of you,' he began, 'I have two lists. The first is of those who have passed your first year – 36 of you – and who are proceeding to second year. The second is of the rest of you, who have failed. Which one should I read out first?'

We agreed that he should read the list of those who had passed. After the professor read the list, he said, 'The rest of you, go study something else – a BA or something.' And with that, he dismissed the majority of the class. He was an impatient man not known for political correctness.

'Right, now a wonderful two-month vacation lies ahead for all but one of you. This person will be required to do extra work over the holidays. Should I read out the list of who is going on holiday or should I read out the name of the person who has to do the extra work?' he barked.

'Prof, just read out who is staying if it's only one name so that the rest of us can go,' I volunteered.

'Right, well, that was easy. Pavlo, you are staying. The rest of you can leave now. Have fun and see you next year. Oh, and by the way, well done.'

The class emptied. Fast. I felt a very lonely figure and then I felt angry.

I approached the professor, who was looking through some documents on his desk. 'Prof, what's the deal? Why me? What have I done or not done to deserve this?' I needed this holiday to get back to Cape Town to fix the family business.

'Now you listen here, Mr Phitidis,' he said, peering at me through his bifocals, 'I have not committed 40 years of care and love to this industry to have anyone fail at my degree.'

Fail *his* degree! I was getting fed up and felt under pressure. I had studied hard, written the exams, paid my university fees, and I had applied myself.

'What I teach here in class is great for corporate employees. I designed the course for those wanting to work for big construction firms. It is my opinion, Mr Phitidis,' he said pointing his finger at me, 'that your personality and attitude are unsuitable to corporate life. That being the case and in order to protect my degree and therefore my reputation, you'll be presenting yourself at my three building sites where you will dig foundations, lay slabs, build walls, install wires and pipes and put up roofs. You see, Mr Phitidis, your unsuitability to corporate life will most likely see you start your own construction company, and in doing that, how do you propose to employ your staff if you have never built anything with your hands first?' He peered straight into my eyes.

I was speechless. He was right. How do you employ and evaluate the performance of, for example, a bricklayer, if you have never laid bricks yourself?

I often share this story with my team. It holds so much truth in its simple logic.

- ❏ Having a good crew to help you sail your ship means getting the right people to do the right thing at the right time at the right price.
- ❏ Often, we hire people in the desperate hope that they will fix some urgent problem in the business. We copy job descriptions off the internet and hope they will get on with it. When we are disappointed in their performance, instead of looking for the real reasons for their failure we simply blame them and claim, 'If you want something done properly, you have to do it yourself.'
- ❏ However, the failure of staff to perform in a business is often more a result of our failure to build systems to enable them to do their jobs. When building an Asset of Value, we build systems before we hire people to operate them, and not the other way around.

- These people are called **system operators**. Their jobs are defined by the activities they will perform in operating a well-built system, and their performance can be measured by how well the system functions.
- People perform at their best when they understand how to do their jobs, why they are making an impact and when they are given autonomy to create value for the business.
- Empower your people to excel in what they do.
- Encourage them to always contribute to improving the business's systems by giving them control over what they do and reinforcing that they are making a difference in the lives of others through their work.

Chapter 8

Your Time

'You may delay, but time will not.' – Benjamin Franklin

What is the most precious commodity in the world? The one that is depleted every year, month, week, day, hour, minute and second?

The answer is your time. It is something you can never get back.

And who is the most expensive resource in your business? The one who stands the most to lose if the business fails? The one who is the deepest repository of knowledge and know-how? And the one with the broadest and deepest understanding of the business and who holds the decision-making power to act on opportunities or threats?

The answer is you, the business owner.

Given this fact, how do you spend your time? Do you spend it running between the bridge and the engine room? As business owners, because we are always working on, thinking about and busy in our businesses, we seldom pause to understand how to quantify and value our time.

Jack was feeling good. The grind of building his System of Delivery was mostly complete, although building and fine-tuning a System of Delivery is not a finite exercise and requires ongoing attention – it must always be tweaked and adjusted to match the growth of the business and the changing environment.

Manufacture time to focus on growth

'How are you spending your time nowadays, Jack?' I began as we sat down for our breakfast.

He raised an eyebrow and smiled, and I knew that breakfast would become brunch.

'Do you remember how I was feeling about the business when we first met, Pavlo?' he asked.

'Remind me,' I said, deliberately wanting to recall the emotion of our first sessions.

'It was horrible. I hated what I was doing and felt so defeated. I remember starting so many things and not finishing them by the end of the year. I carried a terrible sense of self-doubt and defeat. I felt drained, exhausted and burned out.'

'What's changed since then, because that's not the person I'm having breakfast with today?' I prodded.

'Definitely not.' He laughed. 'Back then I was involved in all aspects of the business every day. Or so it felt. From sales and marketing to operations and finance, it never stopped consuming me with daily, weekly and monthly activities. I was in constant operational mode, supporting staff, dealing with customers and suppliers and putting out fires: busy – so busy being busy. It's all I remember and I used to think that this is what running a business is all about. I used to think that busy-ness was business.'

It's the lack of clarity of purpose and direction that erodes our potential and confidence, I thought to myself.

'Today, things are different,' Jack continued. 'It's almost as if we have manufactured time; time I never had before. So, mostly, I spend my time on the bridge and no longer in the engine room.'

'How much time do you spend now, for example, on marketing?' I asked.

'Look, I know it's vital and your obsession with lead-generation is right,' he began defensively, thinking I was going to bang on again about the marketing system. 'Because our purpose is clear, the marketing system we built is simple. Musa is a great marketing system operator. She has a passion and affinity for it. The system works well and she's doing well as a result. All I do is look at the dashboard you built for us and ensure that the numbers are on point – 78 hotel groups; 312 emails to the buying influencers; and between 16 and 23 enquiries for sales closure a month, depending on the season. That's it. It only takes up about two hours of my time a month.'

Goosebumps shivered down my arms like a Mexican wave. Jack's words were as sweet as honey to me. Jack's numbers also showed that sales, operations, procurement and other systems of the business were healthy and performing well. Jack was now the captain on the bridge of his ship. He used the indicators on his dashboard to determine whether the ship's critical systems were operating effectively. There was no need for him to run up and down tight stairwells from engine room to bridge to decks to navigation room and back again. It's clarity of purpose that turns time 'spent' into time 'invested' and only one generates a return.

We ate the rest of our eggs Benedict in silence. I avoided ordering a croissant because I knew that if I did he would've spent the rest of the meeting in soliloquy critiquing the croissant on its construction, texture and taste failings.

As we finished breakfast, I confirmed, 'So, with your time freed up, we are now going to talk about accelerating your business's growth. I have your latest numbers but can only look at them next week. In the meantime, think about how and where we are going to double up on your revenue.' With Jack now on the bridge of his ship and his System of Delivery and team in place, we had built a solid foundation for scaling his growth. We could now press down hard on the accelerator.

Choose to make time to start building systems
Our clients at Aurik are genuinely committed to building their businesses into Assets of Value, but many feel they don't have the time to act on it.

They often say things like, 'We just need to finish our financial year-end,' or, 'Once I have done this deal, I'll get to it,' and, 'The timing is just not right.' I never doubt that business owners are busy. I know: I've been there, and I see it daily. It is a felt reality, but it's also an excuse.

We all have the choice to respond to the world or to get the world to respond to us. We all get to decide how to spend our time. Taking control of your time and turning it into an investment requires self-discipline and deliberate focus. Both are impossible without clarity of purpose, which is in turn impossible without self-discipline and deliberate focus.

Sometimes you need someone to help you kick-start the process to finding and concretising your clarity of purpose. But if you don't make the time to make this investment, you will spend your time keeping up with yesterday, avoiding today and robbing yourself of potential tomorrow.

Responding to the world means the world controls you and your destiny. Getting the world to respond to you places you in control of your time and, as a result, your destiny. Not acting today to reposition your business for growth and success because you are too busy is no different to saying, 'I haven't got the time to learn how to swim because I'm too busy treading water.'

If you find yourself doing the same things and tasks repeatedly in your business, you are trapped in this mindset. To escape from this cycle, you need to step back and figure out how to build systems and enable your team to run them. If you succeed in this, you will be building something structural. This will create the time and space you need to get a new perspective on your business. It will allow you to emerge from the trenches to spot new opportunities.

Spending your time poorly will rust your dreams

There's a further, more nefarious risk in being busy, engrossed in what feels like urgent matters all the time. This is a sure way to lose your love for and reduce the meaning in your work to such an extent that you become an angry, bitter and pinched human being. Jack sought our help at Aurik for this reason. He was driven by his unbridled love and passion for the baking industry to start a business with big dreams and aspirations. It was not the money that made him do it. This is the case with so many of the business owners we work with, who tell us of their love for what they do.

In the tyre business: 'Once you remove a brand-new tyre from its wheel rim and your fingers touch the cold, smooth oily sheen of the rubber of the inside lining, it gets into your blood.'

In the automotive industry: 'Seeing the debris trapped in my diesel filters, knowing that this would've ceased the injectors, excites me beyond belief.'

In the aerial-exploration sector: 'I live for that crisp lidar photo that exposes the topography beneath dense, wild African bush scrub.'

In the data industry: 'Every time I smash the time it takes to process data into a visualisation outcome, I feel alive.'

In the eventing industry: 'When we clear the tech, sound, stage, lights and setup after each event and I see that customers have taken the business cards we left for them on the tables and they call us the next month, I feel humbled, proud, thrilled and scared.'

In the engineering sector: 'Whenever I'm asked to join a proposal to a brief and I ask where the customer found us and they tell me from someone we worked with years ago, Pavlo, the pride I feel and the honour I have in my profession, there are no words …'

In retail: 'Whenever we open a new store and I ask friends, family and old customers what their experience of it was like and they say, "It was just like your other stores," I cannot express the joy I feel in that simple statement.'

The list goes on and I could give you another hundred comments that I have saved over time.

When you are robbed of time to create, time to lead, and time to drive your vision, your passion runs out. Idealism, vital in building a business and being in service of something that gives you meaning, which in turn feeds your energy and drive to persist and endure the long road of building a business, turns sour. When your business turns into a daily slog and the endless noise steals away your ideas and dreams, it's because your time is consumed in the slog and not the dream of why you are doing what you do. Exhausted and worn out, your head and heart generate the defeated thinking and language that translate into behaviour that vanquishes the business in turn.

This is reflected in some of the comments business owners make in our consultation sessions with them:

'I used to love this industry, but now I just want out. I don't even care how.'

'There is so much potential in this business, but you can't

build a business in this country. The uncertainty and people issues will make you fail each and every time.'

But for every business owner who makes these statements, there are others in the same sector and industry who experience an opposite reality. They are growing, energised and only see a bright, exciting future ahead for their businesses. Both can't be right!

Return on time
When building an Asset of Value, your single-biggest expense of time should be on growth. Running a business is very different to growing it. By 'growing it' I don't only mean increasing sales. Growth also includes a number of other aspects, such as creating, testing and experimenting. It means stretching and flexing the business in new directions. It's the fun, trailblazing part of any business that is building momentum. It's the most creative part, built directly off your effort, and it gives you the meaning you long for in your everyday business life. An Asset of Value is just that. It's a business that allows you to focus at least 60% of your time on growing your business.

Act in the present for the future
I obsess about my return on time. I don't measure it against how much money I make. I measure it in relation to the vision I have set for Aurik. I consider where we are today, measure it against that vision and calculate the gap. I then apply a good dose of experience, recognising that all things take two or three times longer than my optimism expects and then quietly

freak out. It jolts me back to my purpose, which is to build a business to fulfil that vision. It serves to focus my attention on what I'm doing and whether it's going to add momentum to my vision. This technique works for me, personally. I also have the great privilege of working with business owners such as Clive and Jack every day. The work I do heightens my attention to time and the consequences of not ensuring that it's being put to good use.

- **Time** is the business owner's most precious resource. How you spend it will determine your success in building an Asset of Value.
- Many business owners complain that threats and opportunities seem to appear out of nowhere. This is because they are too busy, stuck in the engine room, to see the opportunities that pass by and threats that appear.
- When all your time is consumed by the daily grind of running your business, your passion, drive and vision will run out.
- In order to make more time for yourself, you need to build systems and enable and empower your team to run them. Your next task is to use your time to focus on **accelerating growth**.
- Instead of letting your business run you, take control of your time, turn it into an investment instead of an expense, and lead your business from the bridge of your ship.
- Urgent matters are the business of the engine room; important matters are those of the bridge.

Chapter 9

Accelerating Growth

'Go fast enough to get there, but slow enough to see.'
– Jimmy Buffett

Although Jack had been through a rough six months since our conversation about solving his human-resources problem – our 'people conversation', as he termed it – his Asset of Value was taking shape. His System of Delivery was working well, and he had identified great system operators to lead each system. Having moved from the engine room to the ship's bridge, he now had more time on his hands to focus on his business's growth.

I had just finished a meeting when Jack called. He was in a congenial mood. Chatty, if you will.

'Have you ever been to Vietnam?' he asked.

'I have and loved it,' I replied. The country is entrepreneurship in manifestation. Everyone is busy, all the time, non-stop. Nobody hangs about. It has a remarkable energy as a result. 'Are you thinking of going to Vietnam, Jack?' I asked.

Accelerating Growth

'Yes, I'm thinking of taking some time off and holidaying for a while. I feel I deserve a break,' he answered sardonically.

'Nice,' I said, noting his tone. 'How long will you be gone?'

'A few weeks. Okay, six weeks, so that my wife and I can see the country properly.'

I almost had an accident. 'That's not the deal we had, Jack,' I spluttered down the line, and without a beat, I added, 'I have been looking at the numbers again, Jack, and …'

Before I could finish, he said '… We have a problem. I knew you would say that. In fact, I'm sure you will always say that.'

We agreed to meet for a session the following week and before Jack confirmed his sabbatical. Sales growth had begun to slow. Jack's business was reaching a maturity level in the hotel sector for no other reason than that he had a dominant share. And Jack's call was enough of a signal to assure me that the time was right for a big move; rather than touring Vietnam, I had other plans for Jack on how he could spend his time.

Next-level growth

I got straight down to business when Jack arrived for our meeting.

'What's the biggest risk that your business faces today, Jack?' I asked before he even sat down.

'Hi, Pavlo,' he answered.

I smiled.

'Well, it's no longer me,' Jack said. 'My System of Delivery is purring, my customers are happy again – as you can see in our sales numbers – and my team is shining. All my system operators are top drawer.'

While Jack spoke, I brimmed with pride and fondness at the language he used to describe his business. The words you choose affect the way you think. And the way you think determines how you behave, which in turn dictates what manifests in your life and business.

'What about the country?' I prompted.

He paused for a bit and then asked, 'The country? Do you think there is a problem in the country?'

South Africa was preparing to host the 2010 FIFA World Cup. There was much excitement and pride flooding through the country at being the host nation, but there were early signs that South Africa was heading towards a recession. Excited by the event, concerned about its cost and interested in its medium-term impact, I had read extensively about the aftermath of World Cups. Events such as this and the Olympics had not left a positive legacy of economic growth in their wake. Not even remotely. I could not see how the World Cup would be any different for South Africa. I shared my views with Jack. The World Cup would be very good for his business, however, with all the hotels chock-full.

He looked at me and sagged. 'You're right. If there is a problem, I'm deeply attached to the tourist industry!' he blurted out as he sat up straight in his chair.

It is a great position to be in when you can start to think like this, about the big socio-political issues that can affect your business. It's a very clear indicator that you are working 'on' your business from the bridge as opposed to 'in' it. It says that you are driving your business as opposed to being driven by it. We considered a few worst-case scenarios for the country and the tourism industry, something that Carien, who eagerly participated, is annoyingly skilled at.

What if the World Cup would be a disaster for tourism due to crime and other issues that were being debated extensively in the media, such as our stadiums not being completed in time for the event? What if the tourists visiting our country would find better value elsewhere and tourism slowed? What if political maladministration created bureaucratic barriers to tourism, for example by introducing exorbitant visa costs and prohibitive travel regulations?

Instead of going through a process of identifying all the risks that we could face and then doing a probability analysis on them all – a job any business advisor or consultant would cherish – I wanted to divert the session to action instead. Having prepared for the meeting and being determined to cut the length of Jack's holiday down to a reasonable two weeks, I challenged him to think about additional sectors his business could serve.

'Pavlo, it's not that hard, actually; there are many other customers we could start selling to,' he responded.

'No doubt, Jack, but let's agree the criteria for identifying them first.'

'Sure, here's my criteria: they must want freshly baked goods, and they must want the best croissants in town, too.' He smiled mockingly.

Jack knew as well as I did by this stage that the quality of his croissants mattered less than the way his business was built. But our constant sparring and the tone we used to engage with each other allowed us to speak plainly and directly, which was vital in the progress we had made to date.

'Sure,' I moaned. 'But we must let the purpose of the business guide us in finding new customers. These customers need to be in clearly defined sectors and industries. Also, taking them on must not necessitate extensive changes to your System of Delivery and team. Finally, and this is completely non-negotiable, they must want the best croissants in town.' I smiled in compromise.

'I agree with you that the business's purpose must lead us in identifying customers, Pavlo, but I'm not convinced that we won't have to make considerable adjustments to the System of Delivery and team.'

'Just think about what you have today, Jack. Your System of Delivery and team are the engine and crew of your ship. Sailing is smooth and consistent. You are up on the bridge. It's because of this that you can take the time to really think about what kind of customers you want to get on board,' I replied. 'When your business was only focused on selling quality products and services, your customer was whoever wanted great freshly baked goods. And you said yes to every opportunity that came your way. When your customers wanted flour, you invested in silos. When they wanted baking systems, you invested in Macadams. And when they wanted your croissants, you built coffee shop-bakery stores.' I paused, facing an unconvinced-looking Jack. 'This increased the complexity of your operations. Remind me again of how you started the business all those years back.'

'You know the story, Pavlo. I've told you a hundred times.' Jack's patience was fading. I could see he wanted to get to the point. What mattered more than me sharing my views on this issue was that Jack had to realise for himself why the criteria for growth mattered. I had to take him back to the long, hard hours that it had taken him to build his business, completely under-capitalised, from the start.

'I said yes to every customer enquiry because we needed the cashflow,' Jack said. 'There was no money and my start-up capital for the business was driven by trading – you know, buying and selling.'

I could see the memories flood back.

'Hell man, Pavlo, I was delivering croissants and other baked goods from my outsourced, contracted baker to people's private homes to make payroll at the end of the month!'

I didn't know about that, but I could well imagine it. As Jack continued reliving the early years, the stress and exhaustion almost immediately began to appear on his face. It was a torrid time and one that affects most business owners for the rest of their lives. The scars of surviving the first five or 10 years can impede the progress, development and growth of your business forever. Stepping up and beyond the habits developed during those times is hard to do. Failing to do so will limit your opportunities, the business's growth and your personal development.

I let him finish and we paused for a while. His 'job of work' as a trader, driven by survival, had to change. His 'job of work' today was that of a builder, an architect, and it was solely focused on building an Asset of Value. I was determined.

'Why am I here with you right now, Jack?' I asked.

He looked at me quizzically. 'Huh? What do you mean?'

'Okay, so look, I like you. I have got to know you and I believe in you. Of course I do. I'm not here for the money. While that is important, it's more than that,' I began.

Jack settled back in his chair; he could see I was becoming preachy.

'I am driven by Aurik's purpose alone. Success for me is more than the growth of your business, be it in revenue, jobs, opportunities or other ways. Yes, of course that matters. It's vital. It's critical. It has to happen. But it cannot happen at any cost. Growth for the sake of increasing your turnover is not growth for the sake of building an Asset of Value. Growth that drives complexity is unstrategic. It'll unwind all the efforts you have made to simplify your business, to get it sharply focused and sailing smoothly. It'll destroy the beauty we have created.' I finished, leaning back in my chair.

'Now you see what it's like when you tease me about my croissants,' Jack laughed. 'You are no different with your Asset of Value.'

I had just been bust. He was right, the pot had been calling the kettle black! We agreed to Jack keeping his holiday in Vietnam to two weeks.

Accelerate your growth off the back of your established positioning and systems

Five weeks later, Jack called. I had just returned from travelling, and hadn't seen him since our last meeting, but I knew he was busy working hard on finding new customers.

'Hi, Jack,' I answered.

'I need you to come with me somewhere,' he said curtly.

'*Hi, Pavlo, how are you?*' I mocked. '*How was the US, Pavlo, did you have a good trip?*'

Jack corrected himself, 'Hi, Pavlo, how was your trip?' But before I could answer he rattled off, 'So, I'll collect you on Friday at 11am then?'

'Sure, Jack. Where are we going, and what's up?' I resigned myself to his impatience and insistence.

'You'll see,' he said. 'Just trust me. It'll blow your mind.'

Jack collected me from Aurik and we drove out to a grocery store. I knew that this must have something to do with him finding a new way to grow his business. It was a medium-sized store of about 1 500 square metres and part of a franchise. We parked and entered the store. It had a classic design – a rectangular shape with the checkout tills at the entrance and exit and long rows of stocked shelves, with the bakery, deli and butchery at the far end. Above the entrance there was a mezzanine-level office with one-way glass. We were greeted by a cashier who led us up a flight of stairs to the store owner's office.

'Hi, Andrew,' Jack greeted the owner, shaking his hand, and then he introduced me to him.

Andrew invited us to sit down in two mismatched chairs in front of his desk. His office was like a ship's bridge. He had a full view of the store from the tills right to the back and, through the one-way glass, he had his eyes on everything. Andrew's desk was covered in piles of papers and brochures, and on it there was a half-full ashtray, a pair of binoculars, which he used to look over the store, and a computer.

'Coffee, coffee?' Andrew asked, looking at Jack and then me. Without waiting for an answer, he called to his assistant: 'Gladys, three espressos please. And bring some shortbread.'

An awkward silence followed. Andrew was looking at the shop floor from his bridge. Jack was smiling, savouring the awkwardness and wanting me to break the ice, even though I had no idea why we were here.

'So, Andrew, how is life and business?' I ventured.

He turned to look at me, seeming to consider me for a second. 'My wife hates me,' he said, looking me straight in the eye, taking out a cigarette. 'After 40 years of marriage, my wife hates me.' He lit his cigarette, took a deep drag and exhaled.

There was a long, awkward silence. Andrew continued scanning the shop floor for what felt like a long while. The silence didn't seem to bother him. Thankfully, the coffees arrived.

'Gladys, go tell Joseph to sort out the merchandising of the cleaning products in aisle four. It looks terrible,' Andrew said.

Gladys left without answering. We looked on in silence as she went down the stairs and spoke to an employee on the shop floor. With his cigarette in one hand and a coffee in the other, Andrew glared at who I thought must be Joseph, who looked up at the office in consternation before scurrying to aisle four.

I picked up my espresso, quietly struggling with the cigarette smoke. 'Why does your wife hate you, Andrew?' I finally asked, cutting through the discomfort. I sipped at the espresso.

'She's fed up with me for leaving her in a cold bed every morning,' he retorted.

Oh no, where's this headed? I thought.

Andrew continued: 'You know, Pavlo, I get up at 5am 365 days a year to open my store at 5.30am to allow the bakers in. I have to do this so that I can be sure I have freshly baked goods on my shelves before we open at 7am.'

Jack could not hold back his smile.

'In my business,' Andrew continued, 'I only break even on the costs of running the bakery after the 26th or 27th day of the month. Every day, there are three main trading periods for the bakery: morning, midday and evening. The bakery only begins to make me a profit in the last three or four days of the month. My wife hates me because she is tired, after 40 years of marriage, waking up to a cold bed in the mornings.'

Running a bakery is a competitive, low-profit margin business, and Andrew's store was wedged between two franchise grocery stores.

'Besides your wife being fed up with you, Andrew, what other problems do you have? For example, with your bakery?' I asked, trying to discover more about the reason for our visit here.

'It depends on what my staff did over the weekend.

Sometimes they pitch up for work; sometimes they don't. Sometimes they arrive with a babalas and then get the mixtures wrong. Late freshly baked goods on my shelves are of no value. People need to get to work and so they rush in and if your bread and croissants aren't ready, they go to my competition and I lose out.'

It felt like this visit to Andrew was a throwback to the first meetings Jack and I had with his hotel-group client. The same problems were being articulated but in different words. These were the very problems Jack had built his business to solve for the hotel groups. By now, Jack was grinning from ear to ear. I had tasked him with finding new customers without having to change his System of Delivery extensively, and it seemed he had spent his time well. He would supply all of Andrew's freshly baked goods for him, every day, just as he did for the hotel groups, only now he would have to make provision for different goods, such as the frozen cakes and other items that Andrew stocked. This would solve Andrew's problem of having to rely on unpredictable baking staff, and it would allow him to spend more time at home in the mornings with his wife.

Support your system operators but don't micromanage them
Andrew agreed to let Jack run a pilot project to supply him with his freshly baked goods. Pilot projects are a big investment but they are worth doing if there is real commitment from both the supplier and the customer. Adding new products to meet Andrew's demand, over and above those Jack was baking

for the hotel groups, did not stretch his System of Delivery much. Jack had the recipes, his baking lines were geared to support their production, and the cost of baking them was not significant. Jack only needed to make slight adjustments to the System of Delivery, and it only took him a few hours to retrain his system operators. It was a good bet and a great potential investment.

Jack's direct hand in adapting the systems pulled him back into the engine room. It was the right thing to do. He had to ensure that with all the changes the purpose remained clear: to solve his new customer's problems. As the captain of his ship, he also had to ensure he supported his crew and made all the tough decisions. All of these decisions had financial impacts. Jack had the time to think about it, figure it out, support his system operators in the changes they wanted to make, adjust the processes, watch for mistakes, learn from them and make further changes.

But sometimes Jack got too involved in the processes and micromanaged his system operators, not trusting them enough to deliver results. We fought often about this. Being a hands-on man, having built his business from the ground up, Jack's temptation was constantly to jump in, boots and all, tread on everyone's toes and get it done the way he wanted to do it.

'But why can't I just do it?' he pleaded with me.

'Because that's not what we agreed to, Jack,' I answered. 'Let me remind you, we are building an Asset of Value. That means all the hard work you have put into getting a good team on board needs to be respected and trusted. Your system operators are capable people. They have all delivered big time over the years. They are all aligned to the purpose of the business and they all want to take full responsibility for their systems. Let your people be stars. Let them achieve and create. Let them lead. It'll pay you dividends for the rest of your life, dammit!'

I said this knowing how hard it is to let go. To trust. To see something being done differently to how you would do it. I said this having paid the price for making similar mistakes myself. Adopting the mindset needed to operate an Asset of Value almost independently of yourself is easier said than done. Climbing back into the engine room like a control freak is no different to being a bull in a china shop. The work you have done to empower the business and your leadership teams to do what they do best will be damaged.

'So then if I can see that someone is doing something wrong, do I just keep quiet?' he fought back. 'Because let me remind you, I'm the one who carries the cost of that f***-up.'

'Let me tell you a story, Jack,' I began. 'Think back to …'

'I don't want a story. I want to get things done and I want to do them my way. You have always said that my level of care, perfection and obsession cannot be expected of anyone else in my team. I cannot afford to have this messed up. I have built a good relationship with Andrew, and I looked him in the eye and shook his hand on this deal. It cannot fail.'

'Jack, sometimes we have to make mistakes in order to learn from them. Empowering your system operators also means you can delegate as much as you want and should to them. Your team needs to own the System of Delivery. Sometimes they have to learn by trial and error in order to fine-tune it according to their own understanding and behaviour. Your job is to let them fail but to be there to limit the extent of the failure. Small failures, Jack, will cost you only a few rand and cents but gain you competence, independence and ownership in your team. It's a small price to pay and you must pay it because that's what an Asset of Value is all about. Big failures are avoidable if you break the risk or size of the project into small steps. You have to be there to lead from behind and not from in front.'

Always grow with the support of your System of Delivery

Your next growth strategy must be determined by how well your System of Delivery will be able to support its implementation. If you have to adjust more than say one or two out of every 10 processes or activities in your System of Delivery in order to support this growth, the contribution of your new business revenue to profit will most likely be minimal. It takes time and investment to establish the System of Delivery. We all know how hard it is to make small operational changes. For example, something as simple as ensuring the air-conditioner is switched off at Aurik at the end of every day takes time and energy. Yes, I know, we should have smart offices but we don't. Yet!

Here is an analogy that illustrates how chaotic and difficult it can be to change the System of Delivery.

There are two basic methods of fishing in the open seas: trawl fishing and bottom fishing. Trawl fishing involves pulling a fishing net through the water behind a boat to catch fish.

Bottom fishing involves attaching bait to a hook on a fishing line, which you sink to the seabed to catch fish.

These methods are very different. If your System of Delivery is built to support trawl fishing and you want to start bottom fishing in addition to trawl fishing, the cost, investment and chaos that will result in transforming your systems will be enormous. You will have to retool the business in its entirety. In addition to nets, you will now need fishing rods, fishing lines, bait, hooks and sinkers. You will need to train your fishermen to use different tactics and equipment. Instead of preparing the nets only, they will now also need to know how to prepare fishing rods, locate the fish and reel them in. This will disrupt the flow of your business, and either result in failure or an unprofitable business.

As obvious as this sounds, the number of business owners we work with at Aurik who find themselves in this position is remarkable. Sometimes it's not easy to see the obvious on your own, and you need a trusted and experienced mentor to point it out to you and guide you through it. Any growth strategy needs to identify only opportunities to solve customer problems that are deliverable by your System of Delivery. Jack found this kind of opportunity in Andrew's business, and within the week his pilot project was up and running and he was supplying goods to Andrew.

Sometimes business owners get this wrong even after first

succeeding. I'm reminded here of Patrick. He had built a business in the construction industry and found a niche, positioned himself well and built a good System of Delivery to support his operations. He was doing well, better than most in this sector. He fell prey to a lack of discipline that led to a change in focus and saw him turn an Asset of Value into just another construction business.

Patrick – Persistence in positioning is key to sustaining growth

Patrick stood in the doorway of the meeting room. He had arrived early and this was to be the pattern of our engagements. He was lean and tanned, with the sleeves of his company-branded shirt rolled up above his elbows. A master artisan carpenter, his hands and arms were strong and worn from physical, outdoor work.

'Patrick,' I said, shaking his hand, 'I'm pleased to finally meet you.'

He smiled broadly and his eyes were lit with excitement. 'Ja, it's been busy, you know. The economy is tough, and budgets are tight. This has kept me running between jobs and constantly putting out fires but we have to do what we have to do!' He grinned.

Patrick's business operated in the messy, highly competitive construction industry. Thanks to its project-driven revenues, it's a tough industry to build a sustainable business in, even in a good economy. The margin of error is small and mistakes are costly. When business owners in this industry win a project, they are drawn back down into the engine room to deliver it, and as a result it is difficult to constantly identify opportunities. This seemingly endless stop-start cycle ravages the owner's ability to grow a sustainable business.

'This horrible economy is hurting our sector,' Patrick said earnestly. 'The big firms start looking for work downmarket and the smaller firms all cut prices. Clients know this and play them off each other and I am seeing many smaller firms die every month. And when you do get work, the client's scope creeps up all the time and they use payment to hold you to ransom.'

This is a problem in all project-driven work. Clients ask for more than what was quoted on or even change their minds about what they want while still expecting you to deliver the new job at the same price. It's hard to say no because this sours relationships and reduces the chance of referrals, and waving a contract about, claiming that you will have to charge over and above for extra work, is equally difficult.

'I've been in business for 11 years,' Patrick continued. 'People I've done work for constantly refer me to clients. This makes the construction industry's bad reputation work in my favour, big time!' He smiled.

Patrick's business was generating nearly R52m annually, an impressive number for a private contractor.

'Patrick, your business is doing far better than most,' I said.

'Thanks, Pavlo,' he replied modestly, 'but it comes at a big cost to my family and me. I need two things from you guys. Firstly, I want to grow, but I'm scared to do so. Every time I grow, the chaos grows and with that, my life becomes hell. It's already hard to hold things together. So, secondly, my growth must come with order and structure. This running from project to project, having issues with people, fighting with suppliers for pricing and delivery on every job and then battling to get paid by clients, does not make for a good life.'

Patrick was not complaining. Nor was he ungrateful for the work that he had. He simply wanted a better way to do things.

'So, you want to grow, but you want simplicity, and you need more time away from the slog and grind of the business?' I asked.

He looked down, almost guiltily. 'Is that a fantasy?'

'No, not at all. Structure determines behaviour, so you can build your business to give you what you want, but it's going to require making very difficult choices,' I replied with trepidation.

Patrick was the problem. He was charming, engaging, trustworthy and extremely capable. Even after years in this difficult sector he was neither cynical nor bitter. My big concern was that his portfolio – which included building homes, garages, small blocks of flats, reservoirs, small shopping centres, and doing alterations and renovations to residences – was too broad. I got the sense that he could literally build or fix anything. The irony of it all was that Patrick, as a master artisan, was, from the perspective of his business, a jack of all trades and master of none. He served anyone, anywhere with anything related to construction, and this resulted in the chaos he was now trying to escape.

We finally agreed to relook at the structure of the business, ignoring his skills and capabilities, which would generate a service mindset, as well as his historic projects, which would generate a project mindset. We needed a clean slate. We needed to adopt a problem-definition mindset towards his industry.

Over the next two years, Patrick reshaped his business. We had decided to position it almost entirely in the residential sector. Investors and players in the construction industry thought this was insane. Home and property owners looking to build or renovate are price sensitive, mostly disorganised, poor payers and seldom ever happy with building work. They are also hard to market services to.

The terrible economy that had in part brought Patrick to me was now playing in his favour. He identified an opportunity to build loft rooms – which were uncommon in South Africa at the time – for middle-class suburban families under financial pressure. He defined his customers as those who were part of the sandwich generation, carrying the responsibility of providing for children and ageing parents. Patrick created these rooms by transforming an empty roof space into an additional bedroom, playroom, office or storage space. This solved the customer's problem of extending their houses more affordably while still adding capital value to their homes. These customers were also easy to find and market to. Patrick had five loft-room designs, which he was now successfully selling as problem-solving solutions to these families.

'Because a loft room is built into the home in which you are living, the speed of its development is a crucial factor,' Patrick explained to me as we pored over the designs and his portfolio of work. 'It used to take us nearly a month, Pavlo, but today it takes us a week.' He beamed. 'Limiting the number of designs as well as being disciplined on who we service has also let me simplify my supplier base and improve my material costs and reliability of supply. Also, my team has stabilised. Before, I needed people with all sorts of skills to build garages all the way through to small shopping centres.

Today, I have broken up the delivery of a loft room into a system of activities. They are teachable and each person responsible for each activity develops their skills and capabilities on that process every day. Practice is making perfect.' He sat back in his chair and folded his arms.

Patrick had indeed developed a System of Delivery. His suppliers were well organised and reliable. His team knew exactly what needed to be done and when. They also understood the standards that Patrick demanded. His marketing and sales systems were exceptional. Patrick truly understood his customers and the problem they needed him to solve. Most importantly, he understood what experience they wanted in having a loft room built for them in their home. Patrick had what he asked for. A simpler but growing business. One that was dramatically more predictable and one that was becoming easier to manage while it grew.

Just when things seemed to be going well for Patrick, I noticed a change in his business's direction.

'I see a new revenue line in your numbers this month?' I began when we met for our session.

'Where? Oh, that? That was a favour I did for a client,' Patrick said firmly, folding his arms and leaning back in his seat.

'A favour?'

'Yes, a favour. We were building a loft room for a client and he was super impressed with the progress. He then asked if I could build an extension onto his house, a double garage, so he could protect his cars and make space in the yard. So I did it for him,' Patrick looked me in the eye. 'What was I to do, Pavlo? He is a good client and it's a small thing. Can we move on now?'

I let it fly and moved on. Over the next six months, more and more of these anomalies – or 'favours', as Patrick called them – were appearing in the numbers.

The next time we discussed this problem, it turned into a big fight. One Thursday morning, we met at Aurik's offices.

'I want to accelerate our growth further,' Patrick began, 'and I think I have found a way to do it.'

The business was generating nearly R50m in annual revenue. While this was less than it was generating before Patrick redefined his positioning, the business's profitability had almost doubled since then.

'I've been working with another private construction company to build the garages, walls and extensions that my clients ask me to do. I work well with this company and they are doing more or less the same numbers as me.'

'By the same numbers, Patrick, do you mean annual turnover?' I asked.

'Yes, they ...'

'But not profit?' I interrupted.

'No, not profit,' he replied, and continued. 'They suggested we merge and offer a broader range of services to the clients we have. It'll be good for me because I will then be able to service these jobs that I have been getting from my clients with my team already on site. Plus, they have good skills and it would be great to share some of the load and responsibility of the business?'

He had posed the last part of what he'd said like a question. I responded, 'Sell the business to them outright or don't do it.'

Accelerating Growth

'Why?' Patrick persisted. 'I love my business and don't want to sell out. I want to get to the next level and grow further. This is the path, I'm sure of it.'

Accelerated growth requires a solid System of Delivery. Patrick had developed a very well-organised, coordinated, and optimised System of Delivery. His marketing and sales systems were simple and spoke directly to the problem he was solving for his well-defined customers. His operations and procurement operated like well-oiled machines. His costings and administration were simple and consistent. Patrick also enjoyed substantial 60% deposits – rare for the industry – and had collected 98% of the revenue due to him from customers in the three years since changing the business's focus. Patrick was in a position to think about, evaluate, and use data to inform his decision on how to accelerate growth.

'Simplicity is scalable. This means that choosing to accelerate your growth must be measured against the cost of disrupting your System of Delivery. Changing your systems extensively to service accelerated growth will increase your costs of doing business, disrupt the simplicity of your business's design and reintroduce chaos and discord.' By now, Patrick was familiar with the language I used to describe building an Asset of Value, so I added, 'The time you have been enjoying on the bridge of your ship will be no more, and you will find yourself back in the engine room.'

I had begun my defence of his business. I couldn't bear to witness how he would be undoing all the good work he had already done on building his business into an Asset of Value.

I continued: 'Accelerated growth is only of any value if your revenue increases while your costs don't increase significantly. If you make a graph of your revenue and costs, there should be clear gap between them.' I was almost pleading. 'Finally, you are not in the construction business. You are not even in the loft-room building business. You are in the problem-solving business for the families we have identified. And in that business, you want to keep the customer experience consistent and predictable. This deal will mess with all of that. I don't like it and I don't support it. Accelerated growth can come from sticking to your knitting, keeping it clean and expanding into new territories,' I concluded, having delivered my closing argument in defence of my real client, Patrick's Asset of Value.

I bumped into Patrick at an event a year later. He looked at me and away again but eventually came to greet me. The deal he had struck with the private construction company had soured far quicker than he had anticipated. He merged his business with theirs and they changed the company's name. Patrick went on to blame the behaviour of his former partners and conditions in the country and economy for the struggling business he was now in. Something had changed in him, too. The year since we met had aged him, I thought. I also picked up hints of cynicism in the way he spoke, typical of an exhausted and defeated former business warrior.

❏ Once your positioning is clear and you have a dependable System of Delivery and team in place, your next growth strategy must remain aligned with your original positioning.
❏ Similar to how determining your business's positioning

Accelerating Growth

requires focus, **accelerating growth** calls for discipline and being customer-led when identifying opportunities. Don't grab randomly at any chance to grow.

- ❏ Taking on new customers or business must not interfere extensively with your System of Delivery, otherwise you will find yourself burdened with the same chaos in operations that you started out with.
- ❏ Significant changes to your systems will also be costly, and growth for the sake of it is not growth in service of enhancing your Asset of Value.
- ❏ Use the time you have manufactured for yourself to assess growth options wisely. Trust your system operators to adapt and improve the System of Delivery to service new growth.

Chapter 10

Innovation

'The pessimist complains about the wind, the optimist expects it to change and the realist adjusts the sails.'
– William Arthur Ward

One morning, Jack called me to join him for a round of golf. It was almost nine years since we had met, and Jack's business was dominating the hotel sector and generating 12 times his original revenue.

Don't ever invite me to play golf. I'm really good at it and have a hole-in-one to my name. In fact, every time I have played, I have won; in all four of those games I got the highest individual score out of my four-ball.

'What are you talking about?' I barked into the phone, distraught.

'Golf, Pavlo, the game. I need some time out and thought we could play on Wednesday?' he answered.

'That's not the deal we have. We said that Asset of Value was the deal and I'm worried about the business,' I said, having spent the previous week running the numbers over the last nine years. They were both thrilling and deeply concerning. A pattern was emerging that I didn't like. Not one bit.

Break a bit, rebuild a lot, consistently

The business environment is always changing. You need to continually break down certain parts of your System of Delivery in order to rebuild them for the business to remain relevant and suited to the changing environment. These fixes and tweaks are needed to keep your business running optimally. Breaking and rebuilding is also the essence of a resilient, responsive business. This does not mean diverting from your purpose. In fact, it means being led by your purpose. These adjustments must be driven by your purpose or, in other words, by the changing reality of your customers, their problems and required experiences.

Before serving on different ships in the navy, we ran drills on the operating procedures of each ship. We fought fires, repaired hulls, performed man-overboard rescues and did many other exercises to prepare us for sailing. As the size of the ship changed, so the drills, procedures and systems changed, too. They had the same basic structure but were tweaked to accommodate the increased complexity and risk involved in sailing larger ships. Similarly, as your business grows, you will need to constantly invest in making the many small adjustments necessary to deepen and improve its load-bearing capacity and ability to handle complexity to meet the demands brought about by growth. At Aurik we refer to this process as break-build. Although it's a never-ending activity, it becomes easier over time if you have a solid foundation with great system operators in place.

Your costs should not grow at the same rate as your revenues do

'We need to rebuild the hull of your ship, Jack,' I said when we next met.

He looked down at the boardroom table, and for a minute I wondered if he had heard me or if he was distracted by the crack, still slightly visible, that he made in the table nine years ago.

'Let's take a look,' he finally said.

What bothered me was the ratio of costs to turnover. The union of two people through marriage should be celebrated, and the separation of two people through divorce should be lamented. However, in your business, as the upward curve of your revenue steepens, so should the flat line of your costs remain stable: this is a divorce you want to actively drive and celebrate as they grow further apart from each other. Although your costs will naturally increase over time as your business and expenses grow, their rate of increase should be substantially lower than your accelerating sales growth. That gap, the size of that 'yawn', is an indication of success in the design and application of the first three building blocks of an Asset of Value: positioning the business, building a System of Delivery and hiring the right team.

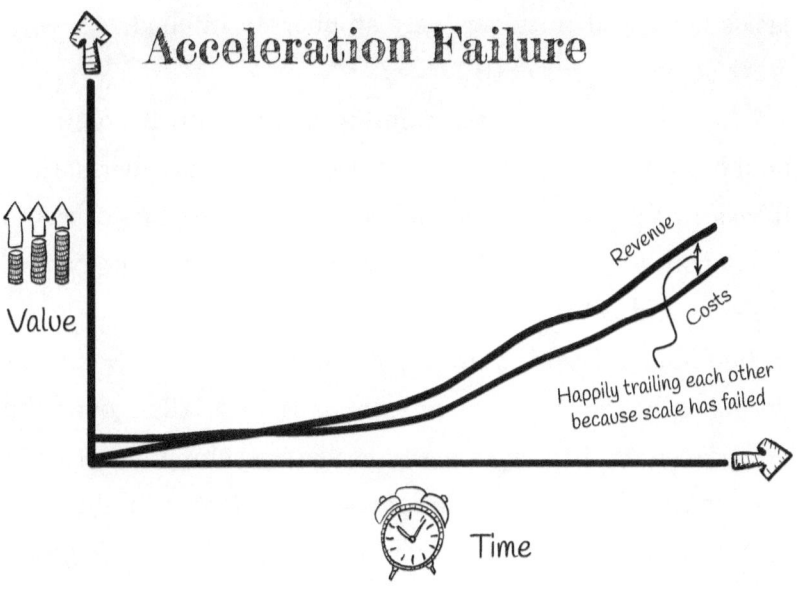
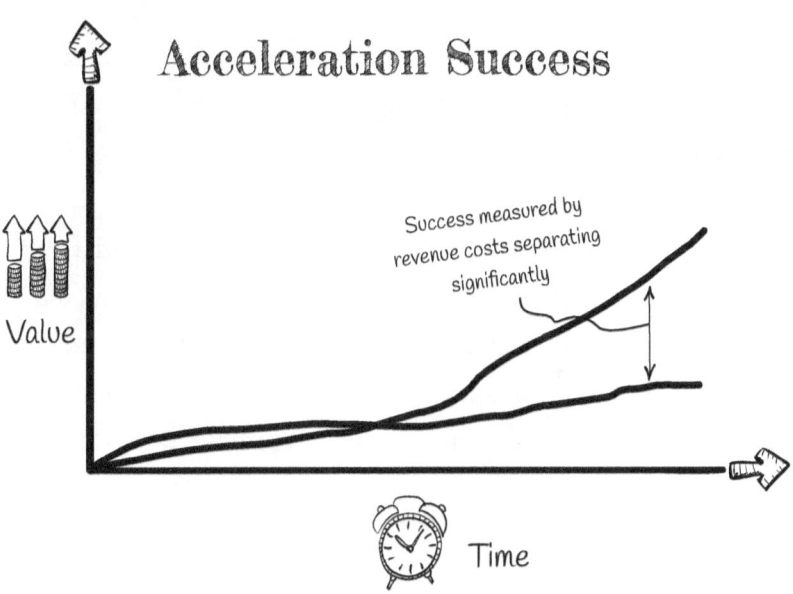

Jack's costs and turnover were stubbornly hitched. As sales grew, so too did his costs.

'There it is,' said Jack, pointing at the culprit cost as if he'd caught a kid stealing sweets from the local supermarket. It was in the logistics and delivery side of the business. As the demand for his products increased, so too did the cost of logistics and delivery to service it.

'Look here,' I said, pointing at the dashboard. 'I was wondering why the sales-conversion rates had fallen over the last year or so. I thought that you were reaching maturity in your market, given your dominance, but now it's telling me something else. Maybe the drop-off is also linked to the growing fleet of vehicles you're operating in order to deliver your products. Fleets are hard to manage and there comes a time when they should be outsourced. It's a speciality business in its own right. Maybe there is a growing discontent building in the customer experience because of something to do with your burgeoning fleet?'

Jack left with his work cut out for him. Because he had a solid System of Delivery in place and a well-versed, motivated team, he had time to focus on such strategic matters. He needed quiet space to gain perspective, collate and analyse data, talk to his team and do what was necessary to understand what the problem was.

We agreed to meet again once he had completed his work, which he did at amazing speed, benefiting from his clear positioning, access to data, solid System of Delivery and good team. Jack's team was so on point it was always thrilling and inspiring to visit them. A business owner's ability to demonstrate this in action to an interested buyer when valuing the business adds a significant premium to the price and paves the way for a clean deal to be struck.

'I've become a f****** fleet-maintenance and delivery business,' Jack groaned. He produced a report that showed how many more vehicles he now had, how deliveries had increased, how accident incidents had become more frequent and how his bills for fuel, maintenance and tyres were stacking up. The consumables were increasing at a suspicious rate and I'd seen this before in several other clients' businesses. Dishonest staff steal fuel and tyres, which they sell for cash, and they use business vehicles as taxis or for furniture removal in order to make some money on the side. What freaked Jack out more were the comments from his customers on the goods-received notes. They were less than complimentary.

Repair or replace the hull while the ship is still at sail
'When last did you visit your customers?' I asked Jack.

He looked down awkwardly. 'It's been some time.'

Two weeks later, we went to meet the same hotel group we had visited together when we were working on Jack's positioning. I was very excited. These meetings were going to be telling.

Jack still had good relationships, though not brilliant ones, with each of the managers at the hotel group. Some of them had left, to be replaced by new employees. Corporate employee churn is a growing trend that is seeing people move and change jobs more frequently than before. It is being driven by, amongst other things, never-ending restructuring, changing skill requirements and slow growth caused by increasing competition. It is rare for people to remain in the same corporate job for five years or more. Maintaining relationships in corporate churn is not an easy task. In relationship-driven business, the saying, 'It's not what you know, but who you know,' only holds true if you are doing once-off deals, but it is irrelevant if you are building an Asset of Value. Regular business comes from consistently solving your customers' problems by delivering the customer experience they want.

Jack, wanting to avoid facing negative answers, mostly asked questions requiring yes or no answers. These were designed to make the problems disappear. It hurts to hear your customers say bad things about your business. As business owners, we are like artists. Our business is an expression of our creativity, and a rejection of it can feel like a rejection of us.

My questions came from a more distant, less personal perspective. They were more direct and open-ended. I did not want to hear answers, I wanted to have a conversation, one that would expose the rising discontent that the data suggested was hidden in the hearts and minds of Jack's customers.

Getting this right, for any business owner, remains one of the biggest challenges. It takes a ferocious, relentless obsession with getting your purpose right and committing to excellence at all costs. Many business owners I speak to deal with rejection by demonising the customer out of pure frustration. 'The customer is stupid,' they say, or, 'The customer is ignorant,' or, 'The client doesn't really care.'

SMBs exist in ecosystems of interdependencies. We are not monopolies, and if we don't give our customers the experience they want they will simply go to our competitors. The way they feel about that experience will outweigh any product, service or price benefits you offer them. And in order to identify how they are feeling, we need to truly listen to our customers. Only then can we resolve the issues.

Each of his customers' comments stung Jack in its own special way.

'Your delivery vehicles are crowding our loading bay every morning.'

'Your drivers are being aggressive to our staff.'

'Your drivers are hooting at the gates at 4am, waking up the guests.'

'You under-deliver stock.'

'You over-deliver stock.'

'Our guests' requirements are changing and your selection of products is unsuitable.'

'Your croissants are not as good as they used to be.' (You should've seen Jack's face after we heard this last one.)

And still we delved deeper.

'We still have our own baking equipment in the hotel's kitchens, and we kept the staff because sometimes your stock does not arrive.'

Each statement fell like a lashing on Jack's body. He winced with each one and his emotions were heaving in tandem with the seemingly growing storm that he was facing.

The environment had changed dramatically. More hotel groups had emerged, increasing competition. Guests were increasingly making their reservations through booking websites as opposed to directly with the hotels. There was increasing pressure to generate more revenue to keep up with rising costs in a market in which price tolerance for accommodation was facing an onslaught by new competitors such as Airbnb.

Jack looked guiltily at me across the table. He had not kept up with his customers' changing environment. It happens, and it's easy, for a minute, to want to take your foot off the pedal. But the environment doesn't relent; it continues to change. The need to be vigilant in order to keep ahead of the market and keep your business relevant to customers never ceases.

Without a System of Delivery, Jack would never have seen the iceberg in the distance. The red light we were responding to was visible to us due to his clear positioning, reliable System of Delivery and great team. Kodak only saw what hit them when it hit them. We were proactively responding to the earliest warning signals indicated on the dashboard by the data generated by Jack's System of Delivery.

We thanked his customers, committed to resolving the issues they had raised and left with a treasure trove. As Jack pondered his internal and external problems, what was clear was that we needed a completely different approach, a creative one that would see Jack gain a new perspective on the challenge.

Innovation

'I'm devastated,' he said in the car on the way back to the office. 'How could I have let this happen? Why did I not see it before it happened?'

'You did. You saw it on the dashboard and the numbers corroborated it. You knew there was a problem and you still have your customers. I promise you that if you solve the new problems your customers will stick with you. They will appreciate that you have identified the problem and have promised to resolve it before it gets worse,' I said with certainty.

'But how did this happen? It crept up on us. I should've seen it earlier.' He continued his pity party for a few minutes.

'Where are you going?' he asked after noticing that we had missed the turn-off to his office.

'It's a celebratory drive, Jack. I want to put foot for a while. Because that's what you have done in the business. You have gone from an eight- to a nine-figure turnover in nine years. We are sailing in a very different ocean. There are bigger predators and your customers are more demanding, buying in bigger volumes and carrying bigger risks. Welcome to the next level!' I said, turning Freddie Mercury up to full volume and clocking a speed that was not legal.

Jack needed time and inspiration. Time to think, away from the business, to explore and think out of the box. Inspiration through seeing new things and talking to people with different perspectives in his industry.

The following week, Jack left for Munich to attended IBA, the baking industry's biggest international trade show. With nearly 1 500 exhibitors to fill his rolodex – yesteryear's version of a contacts app – Jack was resolute on finding a solution to his challenges.

Often, the data generated by your System of Delivery can alert you to changes in the customers environment. Your customers needs may have changed, and they will want a different customer experience in having new problems solved. You can also use data as an early warning system of problems in your System of Delivery. In the same way that Jack used data to identify underlying problems in his business, waste-water-removal expert Themba responded to warning signals on his dashboard to spot weaknesses in his systems as his business grew. Themba used this as an opportunity to innovate and keep up with his customers' changing environment, using technology to address their evolving needs.

Thembalani – Innovating to solve problems and deepen value

'Pavlo, I can't do it any more,' Themba said when we met for a review session. 'I'm run off my feet. I have 230 pumps operating in 13 mine shafts. Never mind the miles and miles of pipes and the number of pumps and valves in play. It's madness. I positioned my business to solve the customer's problem of removing waste water from their mine shafts, ridding them of the costly need to constantly replace their pumps. Instead, I would remove their waste water for them, which they would pay me for per hectolitre. And instead of simply replacing broken pumps, as the mines used to do, I would fix and reinstall my own pumps, but more importantly, I would maintain the system so that we could prevent breakages in the first place. My business was premised on a preventative-maintenance as opposed to a break-fix model, but now it feels like I'm fixing things all the time, being torn from one mine shaft to another, often hundreds of kilometres apart,' he grumbled, embarrassed that he was breaking our covenant, or so he thought.

I could see that there was a problem before Themba said so. It was reflecting in his numbers. Just like in Jack's business, the rate at which Themba's costs were increasing was similar to the rate at which his sales revenue was growing. Themba's business had grown beyond the capacity of his System of Delivery.

'What's worse is that I have been called into a number of meetings with mine managers recently. They are not happy with how things are working and they want me to reduce my price,' he grumbled.

When Themba had positioned his business to solve his customer's problem of reducing costs by outsourcing waste-water-removal, the environment his customers operated in was in disarray, with a long labour strike and downward pressures on commodity prices. Now Themba had to decrease his price by 15%, according to a directive issued by one of the biggest mines in the country. A crisis was on the table and his knee-jerk reaction to it as well as his exhaustion was to sell his business while he was ahead.

'Themba, we did not let the crisis in the mining sector that birthed your business go to waste. Let's not waste this one either,' I said, determined to change his mind. Sometimes a different perspective can be worth its weight in gold.

It was much cheaper to prevent his pumps from breaking than it was to repair them. Because he was paid by the volume of waste water he removed from the mine shafts, the longer his pumps pumped worked, the greater his revenue was. The less often they broke down, the greater was his profit. What a neat business!

Themba's preventative-maintenance programme was managed on a complex spreadsheet. Maintenance teams rotated according to schedules. These teams would go out to inspect the pumps, literally by putting a stethoscope to a pump, listening to how smoothly it was operating and deciding if it needed to be repaired, replaced or left alone. This was one of the biggest bleeds in cost in Themba's business. It was an inefficient system, with teams having to respond to many unnecessary calls along miles and miles of pipes. The mines were also grumbling about having Themba's teams come onto the mine grounds daily and interfering with mining operations such as blasting, clearing and hauling.

I arranged a meeting between Themba and Brian, another entrepreneur I was working with whose business designed and developed internet-of-things devices and solutions. Simply put, Brian embedded computing devices into objects, enabling them to send and receive data via the internet, enabling the user to collect and interpret information on the object and the system it was part of.

We began by collecting months and months of data, trying to identify what caused the pumps to break down. Patterns began to emerge. In the pumps, wear and tear was first experienced in the ball-bearings. Worn ball-bearings began to vibrate and rattle the pump, which in turn displaced fasteners and dislodged gaskets, resulting in other issues. This was great news. I was thrilled, Brian was more so and Themba was full of anticipation.

After some experimentation, Brian built a series of rugged devices that he installed in the pumps, pipes and valves. These measured the intensity of vibrations in the pumps and the volume of waste water flowing through the pipes and valves.

'Right,' Brian said when we next met, 'I can use this data to determine the tipping point for when vibrations in a pump will exceed a certain threshold, at which point the pump is about to break. At this point, you will be alerted by an automated preventative-maintenance call.'

'For real?' was the full extent of Themba's reply.

It took a short while to determine the vibrational tipping point that would trigger the preventative-maintenance call. Further, Brian and his team developed software that enabled Themba to identify each pump and check its individual performance.

After running the new system for four months, tweaking it and optimising it, Themba reduced his crews and vehicles. This process of digitising his maintenance system was only the beginning. More importantly, Themba forgot that he wanted to sell the business.

'I still reflect on that period with amazement, Pavlo,' Themba confessed to me in our most recent session. 'If I was not feeling glum and burned out, if there was no crisis in my business and if the mines weren't forcing me to reduce my pricing, we would not be where we are today.'

I smiled and nodded in agreement. Necessity truly is the mother of most inventive and industrious actions.

He continued, 'Here we are today, controlling my business

> literally through my cell phone. I can tell you in a flash which wastewater-removal lines are working well and which need preventative maintenance. I can tell how much waste water from which shaft is being removed and I can see how much waste-water will be removed this month. My revenues are almost completely predictable.'
>
> 'A smooth, steady ship in a smooth, steady current,' I replied in agreement.
>
> 'You and your ships,' he laughed.
>
> Themba's innovation was a direct response to his and his customers' changing problems. He was still solving his customers' problem, but their customer experience was deteriorating. It was that understanding and the response to it that led to developing an internet-of-things solution for Themba's business. His innovation was led by his customers' experience, not by a great new idea that he or one of his team dreamed up.

Customer-inspired, problem-led innovation

I was so looking forward to meeting Jack upon his return from the IBA trade show in Munich.

'Pavlo, hi,' he said when I answered my phone, 'we need to postpone our meeting. I'm going to the USA. I think I've found something amazing. Something that will change the game completely.'

His tone was unusually measured. He was teasing me and he wanted me to beg. And I did: 'What is it? Tell me ... I've been thinking about the issues since we last met. I have some ideas. What have you found?'

Solutions to problems excite me like very few other things.

Innovation

I can be such a nerd.

'I'll let you know once I have seen it myself,' he said, laughing. 'I need to know it's real and that it can do what was demonstrated at the show.'

I knew it was real already. Changing flights and schedules ... flying thousands of kilometres west ... it was real.

Two weeks later, we met at Aurik's offices. Jack had found the answer. Many, many miles away, out of his box, he had found an innovation in baking technology.

It was called Freezer-to-Oven (FTO). It allowed for producing baked goods to a certain level of completion, at which point it would be frozen for up to three months before being taken out of the freezer and put into a prover (warmer) for a short period of time until it was ready to be served.

The taste, texture, smell and look of the FTO product was the same as a freshly baked version of it ... if not better! Jack made a deal to adopt the technology into his business. It took time and money to implement it. But Jack easily raised the money; securing funding is easy when you can demonstrate that your business is an Asset of Value.

It took Jack a year to adapt his production facilities to support FTO. This required some construction work and reorganising of the production floor. Jack also had to make some changes to his System of Delivery, tweaking it to cater for the new propositions that would be made possible by FTO. What remained constant was Jack's positioning: solving his customers' clearly defined problems through delivering a customer experience they had come to expect from him. This remained his North Star, which he used to navigate his ship through the changing seas he sailed in.

All the while, we kept Jack's major customers close to the developments. They were, in a sense, collaborators in the development of this new offer, helping to give it shape and form. They were just as excited as we were by its discovery.

The hotels had kept their on-site bakeries to cater for special occasions, times when they needed to make changes to their menus or for when Jack delivered supplies late. The average size of these bakeries was 80 square metres, with three or four trained hotel staff – depending on each hotel's circumstances – operating the baking systems.

Jack launched his FTO offering to clients just more than a year after he'd invited me to play golf. It was remarkable. I insisted on joining him in his lead sales meetings for the first month with the bigger hotel groups in the country. I was excited beyond containment and wanted to celebrate an inevitable victory.

We met with the finance managers and proposed a new offer: 'Get rid of your on-site bakeries and turn that space into rentable accommodation; your core business. We will take your baking systems and plough the money back into walk-in freezers and special provers to enable you to order and store a month of continental-breakfast and high-tea confectionery FTO products to meet demand as it arises. One delivery and one invoice every month.'

Innovation

The prospect of new revenues, reduced costs, predictability and reduced waste translated into the finance managers' mother tongue: revenue growth and cost savings. We even managed to get an ever-so-slight, dry smile out of them.

For the food and beverage managers, Jack prepared two options for tasting: freshly baked and FTO products. The food and beverage managers preferred the FTO products in terms of look, feel and taste – a challenge easily won. In addition, they loved the idea that while serving continental breakfast from 6am to 10am they could take the items out of the freezer in small batches, in numbers that would prevent wastage, and prepare these within 15 minutes to serve, filling the dining room with the smell of freshly baked goods.

Jack invited the procurement managers to his new production facilities. He hung his health-and-safety certificates proudly on the wall at reception. The floors were spotless, with crisp lines painted on them demarcating the different stages of production. He kept the inventory stores meticulously. Jack explained that he would take responsibility for training the hotels' staff to his standards in his training facility. But it was the laboratory that won them over. The fact that the lab, responsible for quality control, was scientifically evidenced rather than anecdotally offered, clinched the deal for them.

Finally, Jack offered the human-resources managers: 'With FTO, you can replace your staff of three or four bakers with a single baker, trained at my cost and accredited and upskilled every six months to maintain quality.'

To top it all, Jack offered a free service on data analytics to show consumption patterns, suggest product changes and manage inventory supply in line with seasonal trends. Everyone loved it. Each of the managers would look good in their jobs, too, as a result of Jack's offering. A bakery had become a data business.

Jack reduced his fleet and the associated costs. With deliveries only taking place once a month, he now only needed less than a quarter of the vehicles he'd had before. The cost and aggravation savings were significant. The sharpening of the business focus was even more so. This new model of service and product – let's call it an innovation – was generated by a pending crisis, alerted by data and made possible by Jack having time to think and respond.

Jack himself, the single most expensive and experienced resource in his business, spent his time doing what the leader in any business ought to be doing: leading in response to change. This was going to cement his domination of the hotel sector even further.

A second honeymoon

Within three months of consistent, reliable supply of Jack's FTO goods, Andrew asked Jack to remove the baking equipment in his 80-square-metre bakery and replace it with a prover and a 20-square-metre walk-in freezer, enough to carry a week's stock at a time. Andrew quickly put up shelves in the 60 square metres of freed-up space and introduced more stock that he was sure would increase the frequency of customer

Innovation

visits and the volume of purchases. Andrew worked hard and smart to bring his break-even days down. Each day won was another day of profit.

The cost of the baking equipment, the failed recipes and the hassle of managing unreliable baking staff were all replaced by dependable goods every time and more retail shelf space, meaning more revenue. What's more, the FTO products were baked in batches from 6.45am to 10am, ensuring that they were always warm and that the smell of fresh croissants wafting through the store increased both traffic and sales. I was told that six months later Andrew was going on a second honeymoon.

- ❏ Often, business owners believe that innovation simply comes from them or their staff dreaming up the next big idea, and this idea has little to do with their customers. However, **innovation** needs to be customer-led: it needs to be used to solve customer problems and improve your fulfilment of the experience they want.
- ❏ The customer's environment is always in flux. You need to be vigilant to identify how their needs are changing. Innovate to address this.
- ❏ The data generated by your System of Delivery can alert you to problems in your systems, which can be solved through innovation.
- ❏ If your costs are escalating at the same rate at which your revenue is increasing, you need to find a way to reduce costs while increasing your income, and innovation can help you

Sweat, Scale, $ell

achieve this.

❏ Innovation is enabled by you having time to think clearly and to respond effectively to threats and opportunities.

Chapter 11

The Asset of Value Formula

'You don't have to be a genius or a visionary or even a college graduate to be successful. You just need a framework and a dream.' – Michael Dell

It is important to know how to measure the Asset of Value you are building and to be able to express your interpretation of this clearly.

How do we measure an Asset of Value? The best way is to think of it as an asset that generates wealth for you. An asset holds the promise of wealth creation. Wealth creation requires you to do three things:

1. You need to be able to make money;
2. You need to grow that money through wise investment; and
3. You need to protect that money.

Similarly, your business, as an Asset of Value, must:

1. Generate cash;
2. Grow its capital value so that it'll be worth more tomorrow than it is today; and

3. Be saleable. An asset that you cannot sell or trade in exchange for capital or cash arguably has no value.

To measure an Asset of Value, therefore, we need to determine the extent to which it offers the same features of a wealth-generating asset. Your Asset of Value should become your greatest wealth-generating asset, since this is what you will invest most of your time in.

The Asset of Value formula

'Oh, how I wish there was a formula to life – an easy one I could use to ensure a happy, healthy and wealthy life.' We've all had this fantasy. Wouldn't it be great to have a formula for a successful life, free of troubles and tribulations; something you could apply with little effort or thought to be assured of bliss? In the uncertain process of building a business, formulas offer great appeal in their certainty. They act as a framework to guide decisions and actions and help you chart your course to your Asset of Value destination. They can provide clarity in the noisy, lonely world of business building. So, we at Aurik built one. It's easy to understand and designed to help you keep aware of what you should be doing and when to do it in order to build an Asset of Value.

$$AoV = \frac{A.I}{[P.D.T]^t}$$

The right-hand side of this equation has two parts to it:

The Asset of Value Formula

1. The denominator, or the part beneath the dividing line, is made up of all of the components involved in making money in an Asset of Value – **P**ositioning, System of **D**elivery and your **T**eam, which together free up your time.
2. The numerator, or the part above the dividing line, is made up of the components involved in growing the money made by the business and deepening the value of the asset – Accelerating growth and Innovation.

Let's take a closer look at the denominator first.

[P.D.T]'

P – An Asset of Value has a simple purpose and is **P**ositioned to solve clearly defined problems for specific groups of customers through predictable, crafted experiences. This takes some work to get right, but offers a good return on your efforts and investment. A clear positioning will give you the direction you need to reach your destination. It is also fundamental to a truly customer-centric business.

D – An Asset of Value has a **System of D**elivery that generates steady, consistent sales, supported by reliable and organised operational delivery. A System of Delivery is impossible to build without clear positioning. Even then, it's hard to build, but vision, without hard work, always remains a fantasy.

T – An Asset of Value has a motivated **T**eam with the right people doing the right thing at the right time and for the right price. Invest in your people. Take the time to get this right. A great captain can safely guide a ship through a terrible storm only with the support of a great crew.

t = Having a clear positioning that is supported by a System of Delivery and a capable team serves to release **time** for you as the business owner. It frees you from the daily operational demands of the business to focus on accelerating growth and innovating the business. Without this time, you face the risk of your costs growing at the same rate as your revenue, resulting in the sine-wave growth pattern discussed in Chapter 4.

Getting this part of the formula right takes an enormous initial investment and constant tweaking and adjustment. It will take up all your time and absorb your focus unconditionally. The purpose of this is to make money and release your time to focus on investing and growing that money. Put differently, this part of the formula is designed to get you out of the engine room and onto the bridge of your ship. You need to have it in place before you can move on to the next part of the formula.

A.I

A – Accelerating growth can come from selling new products or targeting new markets, or both. The fundamental rule here is that whichever you decide to pursue, do not let it interfere with, disturb or complicate your underlying System of Delivery. Jack's growth, for example, came from identifying a new customer he could serve with minimal tweaks to his System of Delivery. Accelerating growth must see the gap between revenue and operating costs grow. Break this rule and you will find yourself being hauled back down into the engine room to face growing chaos, with your revenue line taking the shape of an endless sine-wave.

I – Innovation must always support your positioning and be led by the customer experience. Too many business owners try to innovate by coming up with new ideas that have nothing to do with the customer experience. Innovation is not technology. Technology simply provides you with an opportunity to enable elements of your System of Delivery and improve the performance or implementation of your positioning. Your innovation must, like Jack's innovation in implementing Freezer-to-Oven technology in his business, deepen your relationship with your customers. This means innovation must give your customers a dramatically improved experience and more efficiently solve their problems. Any innovation that cannot be tied to these two measures is most likely a fanciful distraction and a waste of time and money.

Getting this part of the formula right promises next-level growth and value for your business, and you can only do this from the bridge of your ship.

❏ The **Asset of Value formula** is given as **AoV = A.I/[P.D.T]**t. This involves determining the extent to which your business generates cash by:
- Being effectively **P**ositioned;
- Having a reliable System of **D**elivery; and
- Having a capable **T**eam;
- All of which frees up your time.

The formula then measures how well you use your time to grow this money and deepen the value of the asset by:
- **A**ccelerating growth; and
- **I**nnovating.

Chapter 12

Measuring an Asset of Value

'You can't manage what you can't measure.'
– Peter Drucker

One of the features of an Asset of Value is that it can one day be sold for a premium price through a clean deal without undesirable terms and conditions attached to the sale. This lilt plays in my mind all day long. I even dream about it every other night.

It is critical for any business owner to understand how business valuation works. How can you know whether you are on course to reach your destination port if you can't keep track of where you are in the deep-blue ocean? And without a clear understanding of how your business will be valued, how will you hope to position your business effectively?

Without understanding how your business will be valued, you are assigning yourself to fate as to whether you will be able to sell your business one day and at what price it will be sold for. This is no different to a captain starting out on a voyage without a clear destination in mind and changing course at the last moment, when it is too late. Taking control of your valuation today means you can act now to ensure a good valuation in five, 15 or 30 years' time.

As we saw with Clive, a business owner could build a business over decades but sell it in, comparatively, a fraction of the time it took to build. You can never get this wasted time back. It is entirely in your hands to take control over how you build your business so that one day you will be able to sell it.

There are many different methods to business valuation. Buyers and sellers use the method that serves their interests best. Most business owners I have met value their businesses emotively rather than by using a formula. They try to put a number on the time, energy and effort they have put into the business. At the end of the day, a business is a complete expression of you and who you are. It's your creative output. And when a buyer suggests a price for your business that was determined using a mathematical formula, you are likely to respond in the same way an artist would to a low offer to purchase a piece of her or his art: 'What, are you nuts? It's worth much more than that!'

The three levers of business valuation

In general, valuation of a business is driven by the returns an investor or buyer can expect. Understanding this puts you in a position where you can build your business to favour valuation and ensure that when you wish to sell, you can maximise your exit price. There are three levers that impact the valuation of a business. Understanding them means that you can pull them in your favour by the way you design and build

Measuring an Asset of Value

your business. Getting this right makes you a price-maker when selling rather than a price-taker. The levers are:

1. **How long your business will be able to operate into the future without you, given its current circumstances.** Without you at the helm, how long will your business be able to continue to operate? This is presented as a forecast and a budget over the period of a year or more. The longer the forecast, the higher the valuation. An average forecast is three years. It is seldom more than five years.

2. **The free cashflow of the business, or how much hard cash the business can generate every month.** To illustrate this, let's use the example of an informal business operating in the cash economy. At the beginning of each day, a trader uses the cash in his till to buy stock. During the day, the trader will sell that stock at a mark-up. At the end of the day, the trader will count how much cash is left in the till. That is free cash. No debtors, creditors, provisions, depreciation or other accounting terms need to be taken into account. In business valuation, this is calculated for each month the business is forecast to be able to operate into the future. The more free cashflow a business has over the period forecast in lever 1, above, the higher the valuation.

3. **The 'risk rate' or 'discount rate'.** Using levers 1 and 2 above, an investor determines the value of a business by calculating how much cash it can generate for the period it is forecast to be able to operate for into the future. However, investors need to factor in that they will not receive this money from buying the business now but will only get

it once the forecast period is over. If they were to receive these earnings at the present time, they would be able to invest this money and earn more from it. For example, if you were to invest R100 today at an annual interest rate of 10%, in one year's time the investment will be worth R110. To calculate the present value of that future investment, you would take R110 and apply a discount rate of 10% to get R100. The discount rate is therefore used to work out the present value of the business as opposed to its future value. This lever is arguably the most contentious of the three used in valuing a business. The discount rate for a business is usually between 18% and 45%, with 18% being considered a low-risk investment.

As captain of your ship, it is up to you to determine how your business will be valued against these three levers. How you design and build your ship today will determine how it is valued tomorrow.

Let's take a closer look at each of these levers in order to understand them better. Although there are many different business valuation methods, these three levers form the basis for the *discounted free cashflow valuation*.

Lever 1: How long your business will be able to operate into the future without you at the helm

So many businesses fail to sell because it becomes evident that the business owner has become the business. These

Measuring an Asset of Value

businesses cannot operate without the owner's constant involvement. If you are the business, you don't have a business, you simply have a job. To make matters worse, your business is a job without the benefits of one. In spite of all your sweat and tears, you are not guaranteed being paid at the end of the month. In spite of carrying all the risk, you get paid last in the month and you have 3am wake-up calls. If this is the case, all you focus on is keeping your job, not growing an Asset of Value. If your business cannot generate free cashflow into the future without your being there every day, you don't have an asset! Furthermore, your forecast will be very short.

If, on the other hand, you have built a business that can operate without you, your forecast will be longer. In determining how long into the future your business can operate, the buyer will factor in how much longer your business can serve its customers and offer them the products and services it currently does. The further into the future that a business can continue to operate, the higher the valuation. But potential alone is of no interest to the buyer. For example, if a business owner argues that the business has a lot of potential to sell into new markets, why would a buyer want to pay you for unrealised potential? Potential that, in order to be realised, will have to come from the sweat of his brow and the bend of his back?

Lever 2: The amount of free cash that the business can produce every month

A business's worth is not determined by the value of the assets listed on its balance sheet. Rather, it is determined by how much money your business can make using those assets. For example, imagine that you buy a tractor for your farming business. It costs R400k. However, you never train your staff to use it. When you try to sell your business, the potential buyer learns that the tractor is sitting, unused, in your shed. In her or his mind, the tractor's worth to the business – in how much cash it could generate by its use in ploughing and planting the fields – would be much higher than R400k if your staff were trained to use it. What is for sale is the cashflow that the tractor can earn and generate in the future.

Lever 3: The discount rate or risk associated with the business

Risk is measured in relation to sustainability, and this means relevance within the heads and hearts of your customers. If you have built a purposeful business that does what it promises to do in the way it promises to do it, your customers will stay with the business after you have sold it, meaning that the buyer takes a lower risk in purchasing the business.

Any business that positions itself using product, price or service advantages carries a higher risk for the buyer. Should a competitor enter the market with better product features and/or better pricing and service, your business's advantages will not last long.

If your business depends on your personal service to customers, relying on your personal charm and charisma, when you sell it and leave the business, your customers will leave with you. The risk will therefore be higher for the buyer.

Measuring an Asset of Value

However, if your positioning is clear and your System of Delivery fulfils the customer experience, then it is the business and neither you nor your products, prices or services that keeps your customers coming back. It's this that makes you different.

It was the way in which Themba solved problems for his mining clients by eliminating their need to keep pumps on their balance sheets, rather than his pumps themselves, that set him apart and made his business more valuable. Because his business was sustainable in this way, potential buyers faced a very low risk in purchasing his business, meaning that his business would fetch a higher valuation.

Now that you understand how business valuation works using these three levers, you can appreciate that smart money buys businesses using the discounted free cashflow valuation method. Distressed owners might moan, 'But what about stock levels? What about debtors? What about my business's physical assets? Shouldn't these be considered in the valuation?' As we have seen, smart money looks for the cash that can be generated by a business, not the numbers that appear under 'Assets' in the balance sheet. That is left for naive buyers and auctioneers. The final valuation of your business will also be determined by how you package it. Like an expensive perfume, the bottle and the box make a big difference in price!

❏ How do you put a price on the business you have built? How do you value something that is essentially a creative extension of yourself?

- Most business owners do this emotively rather than by using a formula.
- However, we use two ways to measure the worth of your business: the **Asset of Value formula** (discussed in Chapter 11) and the discounted free cashflow valuation method.
- The three levers used in the **discounted free cashflow valuation** method are:
  - How long your business can operate without you;
  - How much cash the business can generate every month; and
  - How risky it is to buy your business and what its present value, as opposed to its future value, is.

Chapter 13

Buffett is Buying

'Every battle is won before it is fought.' – Sun Tzu

Warren Buffett, arguably one of the world's best business valuators, is constantly interested in investing in good, solid business. With his partner, Charlie Munger, he has a nose for finding the best businesses to buy. He is obsessed with value investing, a strategy that involves identifying excellent businesses with solid fundamentals for sale at bargain prices. It requires evaluating a business considering its operational capabilities, team and the market. Value investing does not tolerate hype and speculation. Rather, it seeks to accurately predict a business's future prospects based on its past performance.

Buffett's buying expedition leads him to Jack's door. Although Jack is undecided as to whether he wants to sell his business or not, he invites Mr Buffett in for a cup of coffee, and decides to treat the discussion as a negotiation to see where it will lead.

'As you know, Jack, I'm in the market for a bakery, and have visited a number of bakeries over the last few weeks. What makes yours special?' asks Buffett.

The typical response to this question would be related to the bakery's superior products and service. Buffett would have expected to hear responses such as, 'We have the best-quality croissants,' or, 'Our recipes have been in our family for four generations,' or, 'Our techniques draw on the first principles I learned as a trainee baker in Stohrer, Paris's oldest bakery in Rue Montorgueil.' Buffett also expects to hear about the standards of excellence in service: 'I know all my customers and they love me,' or, 'I've had the same customers for over a decade now.'

'Well, Mr Buffett,' says Jack, 'I hope you had good visits and I've little doubt that you have tasted some delicious freshly baked goods. But here's the thing. I think you've wasted your time coming to visit me.'

Buffett looks at Jack, slightly perplexed.

'This business is not a bakery,' Jack continues. 'We are a data-driven, problem-solving, value-adding supply chain solution for fast-moving baked goods in the hotel and supermarket sectors.' Jack goes on to explain that his business only uses freshly baked goods as commodities to solve very well-defined problems through well-crafted experiences for his customers. Furthermore, he achieves this by helping his customers add more value to their businesses, citing examples in both the hotel and supermarket environments: the hotels can now eliminate wastage by using Jack's forecasting and FTO solutions; and the supermarkets compete more effectively because they have more shelf space due to stocking Jack's FTO goods, which also produce a consistent aroma that entices shoppers.

Buffett peers at Jack through his spectacles, his lenses misting up ever so slightly from the steam rising from his coffee. He has done his research on Jack. He already knows that Jack's business is different.

Value investing was conceptualised by Benjamin Graham and David Dodd in the early 1930s. A significant part of their approach was to find under-priced investments, and Buffett is following in their footsteps, looking for a good deal. It's in his blood. Over time, Charlie Munger tempered Buffett's deal-hunting to include the need to identify a good business with a good team.

'I should also mention, Mr Buffett, that I wish I could lay claim to this business. Its design, its positioning in the market and its growth are neither my genius nor my brilliance,' Jack says.

Again Buffett looks perplexed.

'This business is, for want of a better phrase, "public property",' Jack adds. 'It was conceived by and built around the ideas, needs, problems, engagements and conversations I had with my customers. It's not my idea. It's theirs. My idea of a good business used to include, as its only ingredient, great croissants.' Jack smiles mischievously. He wants to drive a wedge between what makes his business special and what makes any one of the more than 5 000 bakers in South Africa special. In answering Buffett's question, 'What makes your business special?' Jack alluded to his **Positioning**, ticking the 'P' box in the Asset of Value formula, already earning his business a premium.

Buffett grunts. 'That's really great to hear, Jack. Well done. Indeed, it's a very different value proposition. Most of the others lauded their croissants,' Buffett says, smiling.

Buffett is a nice guy, Jack thinks. *He's quite charming and funny too.* (Don't be fooled, Jack, he is a master negotiator!)

'But, Jack, I can now see that you are the DNA of this business. It's your heart, head and hands that drive it,' he cunningly continues, flattering Jack all the while.

'Thank you, Mr Buffett,' Jack replies, smiling, 'but you are wrong. I wish that were the case, and it *was* once the case. Today, this business operates off a System of Delivery. I have a remarkable leadership team, with system operators responsible for the six main systems that deliver the positioning proposition to our customers. My team has been with me for some time now. They are all well incentivised and have earned a large degree of autonomy in their domains. They love it here, and while we have grown, this team is as tightly knit as the System of Delivery in the business is. Here, let me show you.' Jack turns his computer screen towards Buffett, who leans in and sees Jack's business dashboard. Each system has its own set of indicators. Jack truly manages his team on numbers alone, and the numbers, Buffett can see, are tied to the performance of the systems in the overall System of Delivery.

'Very nice,' mutters Buffett. His argument – 'You, Jack, are the business, and if I buy the business, I am buying you and you are not for sale' – is fading fast. This argument, the same one used to collapse the dreams of a R42m sale for Clive, is a well-used negotiating strategy.

'As you can see, this business runs without me. Almost!' finishes Jack, with a wry smile. In answering Buffett's question, 'Can this business continue to do what it does without you?' Jack has ticked his **System of Delivery** (D), **Team** (T) and **time** (t) boxes in the Asset of Value formula. His business can function without him for a long time. Certainly longer than the three to five years Buffett was going to use to drive the price down. Jack's business would more likely operate for seven to 10 years without him.

'I like the dashboard, Jack. I see that it also has your history on it to support the forecast you mentioned,' Buffett approves. 'Are you not concerned that you are heavily invested in the hotel sector? If that sector suffers because of some event, it could hurt the business?'

'No, not any longer,' Jack grins. 'We recently, a few years ago, entered into the retail-supermarket sector. As you can see we now own almost 30% of it and the growth there will be substantial. The thing that excites me most about it is that our entry there was based on the exact same positioning we have for the hotel sector. This meant that with a few little tweaks here and there, our System of Delivery, which was developed to deliver a consistent experience to the hotel sector, could deliver a good customer experience to the supermarkets too. The result,' Jack points again to the screen, 'is that the sales line has accelerated while the costs line has levelled out. That gap is our gold.'

As Buffett peers at the screen, the graph shows the widening gap between the revenue and cost lines. Buffett smiles broadly. He knows that his last argument, the question of sector concentration and more specifically, profitability or free cashflow, is beat.

'I love it,' he responds.

'So do I,' Jack laughs.

Buffett has almost run out of points to argue in driving the business's price down. In answering Buffett's question, 'Aren't you too concentrated in the hotel sector?' Jack has ticked the box of **Accelerated growth** (A) in the Asset of Value formula, proving that his business's free cashflow is healthy. This bags him gold status in Buffett's calculations.

Leaning back, as if to conclude their meeting, Buffett looks Jack in the eye. 'One more question, Jack, if I may ...'

'Of course,' Jack replies, wondering what it could be. Buffett seems, in his tone and body language, to have a card up his sleeve.

'What stops any of your customers terminating relations with you? Sure, I understand your positioning and that your System of Delivery produces a consistent, reliable experience for them. But people are people, and they change. What if one of your customers gets a new CEO who just doesn't like your business? It happens all the time.'

'You are right, Mr Buffett,' Jack offers. 'That was a risk.'

'*Was*?' Buffett leans forward questioningly.

'Was,' says Jack. 'Today, our customers are entirely reliant on us. We account for all of their baking needs. They no longer have on-site bakeries, recipes and baking staff. They rely on us and I keep our prices low; we constantly stay out of trouble and sight due to how the System of Delivery works. Our service to them ticks over smoothly, day after day. Take this as I say it,' Jack says, 'they need me more than I need them.'

He's right. They need Jack and he never disrespects the fortunate position he has built his business into. He continues to include and celebrate his customers every year, recognising them for what his business has become, remaining humble in all his engagements.

Mr Buffett nods. 'But how sustainable are your customer relationships?'

Jack explains that what was once a commodity business is now a necessity business for his customers. The innovation of FTO provided his business with a deep advantage when he first led its development in the market. This secured him a place in the supply chain of his customers. His subsequent innovations, all of which responded directly to stated problems being experienced by customers, all led to incremental amounts of value being added into his service. What was once a project-based business, delivering products every day, is now an annuity-based, solutions business; every investor's dream. Through his answer Jack has ticked the **Innovation** (I) box in the Asset of Value formula.

Jack and Buffett move on to discussing the business over lunch.

'I love your business, Jack,' Buffett says.

'So do I,' Jack responds.

'I love its ten-figure turnover, too,' Buffett continues.

'So do I,' Jack replies.

'Is it for sale?' Buffett asks, removing a scallop from its shell after sipping his Coke.

'Not yet,' Jack smiles.

Be warned: the business that today behaves like a Dementor, sucking all hope and enthusiasm from you, holds the potential to, if built right, make a comeback that will surprise you with the force of its potential. The dreams you had starting the business will come back to life, released from being trapped in the design of your business, and shape the reality that will make your business great again.

Every time I support a client in selling her or his business today, I think about Clive and Jack. I consider where the business was, pre-Asset of Value, and where it is now in that transaction. There are so many Jacks and Clives out there. Each is the same, in so many ways. Yet, one may be slightly smarter, slightly luckier, and the other may be slightly harder working, slightly brighter.

❑ If Warren Buffett showed up at your door tomorrow and offered to buy your business, how would you convince him that you deserve a good price and fair terms? Using the Asset of Value formula, you would need to demonstrate the extent to which your business:

- Is a problem-solving, value-adding solution as opposed to a product-, service- or price-centric one;
- Is built around efficient and well-built systems;
- Is run by a great team; and
- Benefits from you having time to focus on accelerating growth and innovation that is customer-led, resulting in the gap between costs and revenue increasing.

Chapter 14

Different Kinds of Business Sales

'It is not the ship so much as the skilful sailing that assures the prosperous voyage.' – George William Curtis

A business sale can take many different forms. The best kind is an outright sale, one that earns a premium price in a clean deal. In order to achieve this, you need to build your business into something special, an Asset of Value that offers much more than competing businesses.

A clean deal means one in which most if not the entire purchase price is paid up front and is not dependent on the business achieving certain targets post-sale. You should also have the option to step out of the business immediately or after a short handover period. The handover should have no warrantees attached to it and you should be compensated for your time in that period at a fair market rate.

Below we will consider this and other kinds of business sales, looking at examples and the main points of each type of sale.

Different Kinds of Business Sales

Outright sale

This type of sale seldom happens, but it is what you should be aspiring to as a business owner. It results from your business being built into an Asset of Value with clear positioning, a System of Delivery, a capable team and an offering that makes your business unique from others. This was the case with Tony, a former client of Aurik whose Chicago-based health-insurer customer-vetting business was sold at a premium price with favourable terms and conditions.

Tony positioned his business to solve his health-insurer clients' problem of taking on dishonest customers who would lie about their health issues or omit important information in their applications for insurance, resulting in the health insurers having to pay out increasing amounts in claims.

When customers applied for health insurance, Tony's business would assess the application and evaluate the applicant's risk level. His business would scour the internet and gather, organise and present data on the applicant. If the applicant left out any of the ailments he or she had suffered from in the past on the application form, or omitted to include any other pertinent medical incidents, Tony would know.

For example, one applicant left out the fact that they had been involved in a fender-bender eight years before. To the applicant's surprise, the quotes he received from the five health insurers he had applied to for cover were higher than expected. All of these five insurers were Tony's clients; all received a report from Tony's business that included details of the accident, online searches the applicant had made for car repairs, the enquiries and visits the applicant had made to chiropractors as a result of being injured in the accident, and purchases on Amazon for back-support products relating to his injury.

Tony had started his business in 1998, but over the last five years since we had met, he had used the Asset of Value approach to build his business, digitising many of his costly administrative tasks and creating a System of Delivery.

When Tony wanted to sell, his biggest customers clamoured to buy. He secured a price upwards of $200m. The terms were cash up front, a three-month handover and a voetstoots ('as is', or without reservation or qualification) sale.

Common sale

This type of business sale happens most frequently throughout the world. It is anything but clean and certain. In a common sale, the seller often has to accept a low price, and there are many demanding terms, conditions, warrantees and penalties attached to it. Clive found himself on the receiving end of an offer to purchase his business via a common sale. As a business owner, you should aim to avoid this.

One of the things Carien and I had to do when listing one of our businesses on the JSE was to buy a number of other businesses and bring them together to demonstrate the vision of the business in action.

We bought all of these businesses through common sales. In each case, we were the price-makers and they were the price-takers. The reasons for this were simple. They all operated in

Different Kinds of Business Sales

competitive markets and we were spoiled for choice in terms of businesses to buy. Their books were untidy, and they were incurring all sorts of expenses that diminished their historic profits. As a result, they had to warrantee their future profits in order to justify the purchase price of the business. Furthermore, they only received a small portion of the price up front in cash, while payment of the majority of the purchase price would be split over three years, subject to the businesses achieving certain profit targets. We further insisted on taking over the bank accounts and consolidating all the administrative functions of each business to increase efficiency, governance and accuracy of reporting. Listing requirements are strict in terms of such matters. Finally, a significant amount of the payment to the businesses was made in shares, on a similar basis to the offer made to Clive.

Recently, a JSE-listed company, EOH, ended an unfettered SMB buying spree that lasted about six years. They paid for the SMBs mostly in shares. In some cases, shares accounted for as much as 80% of the purchase price. When they started this buying spree, their share price was growing and valued at around R150. Today, their shares sit at R14.50. Let's imagine you sold your business to EOH back then in a common sale for R50m, with 80% of the price paid in EOH shares. At the time of selling, you will have received R10m in cash and 266 667 EOH shares worth R40m. Today, your shares would be worth R3.8m, and not including any interest you would have made on the R10m you received in cash, the amount you would be left with from selling your business for R50m would only be R13.8m!

Management Buy-Out (MBO)

The next most common type of business sale is an MBO. In these sales, a deal is done between the owner and a successor, typically the current management in the business. Mostly, the management team borrows money from a funder to pay the seller. They do this on the basis that they have the ability and track record to grow the business further and settle the debt in the future. Carien and I sold three of the 12 businesses we built in our formative years through MBOs.

We had several reasons for doing this. In some cases, we felt committed to the management teams we worked with and wanted to provide them with an opportunity to take control of their own destiny. In other cases, management came up with offers that were compelling and on terms that worked for us.

These businesses were never our core focus; we had developed them to be our first customers in order to understand how to build Aurik itself and fulfil the vision that inspires and motivates us to this day. In each of the three cases that we sold through MBOs, we knew the buyers – our management teams – well and had relationships in place. We knew how they behaved, what kind of people they were, and we knew the businesses well. We did fair valuations and put fair terms on the table. The buyers raised their own funds between themselves and by securing private-equity funding from other investors.

Family sale

This type of business sale is similar to an MBO, but in a family sale, instead of the founder selling the business to management, he or she sells it to a family member. Globally, the rates of success for family succession in businesses are dire. In the formal economy, research shows that only 28% of family businesses succeed in the transfer from founder to the first generation of successors and thereafter, from first to second generation, only 5.1% achieve success.[3] At Aurik, we see these challenges daily, with nearly 60% of our clients being family businesses.

I personally experienced many challenges in taking over the family business from my father, and here I share my story of this with you. After years of running a successful business, my father found it difficult to relinquish control of the business, to be impartial in fixing the leaks that were appearing and to allow the business to grow with the times and in a new direction. I learned some of the greatest lessons in turning the business around, some of which inform my approach today. I discovered that it is never too late to start building your business into one that will ensure your financial security into retirement. But mostly, my story shows that it is possible for family to work together to create a saleable business, and this can be a transformative and rewarding experience that can bring you closer to rather than alienating you from those closest to you.

Sweat, Scale, $ell

The challenges of family succession

Before starting Aurik, I was involved in five businesses. Well, actually, only three of these were real businesses, because in the other two I was the business, meaning they were simply jobs. I was everything from chairman to CEO, coffee maker and cleaner.

Two of my real businesses were failed concerns that I had bought for a dollar each, taking on the debt. I was fortunate to have succeeded in selling both for substantial amounts later. The third real business was my father's, an importer of camping, sports and leisure equipment.

My parents had children late in life and the age gap between me and my father was significant. He was pure sunlight, a man of great largesse and life. He worked hard, was a leading member of the trade association governing the industry he was in and built remarkable friendships through the business. I remember from the age of five meeting his business associates from all around the world. When visiting our home they always brought my brother and me small gifts. We sat with them at the table for meals, and they spoke about their lives in faraway places such as Taiwan, Japan, Czechoslovakia, India, America and Italy. They brought samples and my dad placed orders, negotiated prices and terms and made deals with them.

My dad had customers across South Africa – mostly small, independent retailers. It was a small business that employed 28 people. It was a success, too. My parents, who both worked in the business, bought us clothes, schooled us, fed us, bought us bicycles and took

Different Kinds of Business Sales

us overseas twice on business trips: once to the Far East, and once to Europe. We were privileged and fortunate.

My parents came from immigrant families. Their parents had worked all their lives and the values of work ethic, respect for money and refusal to waste were well entrenched in our family. My brother and I still practise a spartan, protestant work ethic. And we aren't even protestant! That was simply the way of the world as we saw and knew it.

My father was also a proud man. He was clean in thought, loved routine and looked after himself and his family. One evening, when he sat down on the green couch in the lounge, pulled out the paper, lit a cheroot and began to read the evening news, I saw in big, bold type on the front page: 'Sold for just R1'. I stared at it for a while and asked my dad what it meant. All I heard in reply was that a company could be bought for a rand.

How cheap it is, I thought, *to buy a company; one day when I grow up I will buy one of my own.*

It was only after I had bought, fixed and sold my first business that my mother reached out to me. She was deeply concerned about my father.

'What do you mean, Mom?' I asked.

'He has not been sleeping well and tosses and turns at 3am almost every night,' my mom replied. 'His spirit is down, and he won't tell me what's wrong. I think things in the business are not going well.'

She had since left the business and was no longer involved. I tried talking to my dad. But the last thing he wanted was for him and my mom to get in the way of my brother and me following our own journeys, and he didn't want to trouble us with his concerns. This also meant that my brother and I had to carve our own paths in life.

But one day my father said to me, 'You've sold your business and seem to be between things. Why don't you come join me in my business for a while to kill time?' It was a proud gentleman's invitation.

It only took three months for the horror to show itself. Debtors were running over 142 days late, stock-outs were the norm, and staff were sloppy and sluggish. The business was housed over two floors of a building in downtown Johannesburg that leaked in 149 places. I knew this because when I asked what the pile of buckets was for, the storeman explained. All recordings were made on paper. There was no computer to be seen other than my dad's trusty, plug-in calculator. The goods lift only worked half the time.

We had a problem here. The family had a problem here. The many awkward conversions between my father and me over the first three months exposed that the business had financial problems, and this meant that he had financial problems too. Visits from the bank had become more frequent in those three months, further deepening the crisis.

I learned that my dad had tried to sell the business. He could not get anywhere near the price he needed to look after himself and my mom and finish paying for my brother's university education. He swore me to secrecy and refused to let my mom, my brother or any of his long-time friends and colleagues know. His staff suspected that things were not going well, but he had the habit of paying them on time every month, so they didn't say anything. He knew their families.

Different Kinds of Business Sales

I am a very energetic, driven person. I believe that action follows thought, and my patience is short. Duty bound, and out of love and concern, I committed to act on the business. I also relished the challenge. Back then, I believed, and still do believe, that most businesses can be fixed. After all, I had just succeeded in turning a failed business around, selling the business I had bought five years ago for $1 for an eight-figure number.

Also, time was not on Dad's side. The banks made that very clear. I started by looking inside the business. I had to stop the bleeding. I turned to staff and asked their opinions. This was critical. Most of the management had been working in the business from before I was born. I had to build up their respect for what was about to follow. I also needed to learn very fast. With their help, I found the low-hanging fruit quickly. We fire-sold stock that wasn't moving thanks to Herbert, the storeman of 42 years in the business. I called in the 10 longest-outstanding debtors, all of whom had trading relationships with my dad reaching back over 20 years. We got paid shortly thereafter.

Based on these experiences, I could have written an entire book on how to collect debt without ruining the customer relationship! We repainted the walls, forced the landlord to fix the leaks by withholding the rent (this seems to be required to get landlords to behave properly) and replaced the broken windows and lightbulbs. That took two weeks.

Next, I went on a road trip with some of the sales representatives. There were six of them, classic travelling salesmen with economical cars that had large boots filled with bags and bags of samples. I learned quickly what was selling and what was not. I made more notes on further fire-sales. I learned about the different types of customers and what challenges they were facing in building their businesses and simply surviving. I learned which reps could sell and which were just order-takers. This took three weeks and 10 000 kilometres.

Back in Johannesburg, I visited the two banks we had accounts with. In those days, your relationship with the bank manager was more important than it is today. I presented my turnaround plan and in both cases managed to buy us another six months. Over the next week, I spoke to 87 suppliers. There was no money to travel to see them, so the phone had to do. The business carried more than 3 800 inventory units. We needed a refresh. Guided by the customer visits and discussions I'd had with our reps, I needed to start the refresh.

My dad and I were six months into our relationship in the business. Up until then, I had discussed all the changes I'd made with him. He had only objected to a few of these. Now, I needed to make some big changes, so I insisted that my dad take my mom for a two-week holiday to the coast. My dad and I had our first big fight when they got back from holiday. I had completely computerised the business. I had bought four computers and a dial-up modem, and set up accounting and inventory software. My dad found himself isolated from his business overnight. His treasured routines were stolen from him. The ability to check the handwritten invoices, cost out new stock with his plug-in calculator and make buying decisions based on gut feel rather than inventory stock-turn data were all gone. The routine that gave him meaning and purpose, which made him feel in control of his business and life and that built his self-esteem, disappeared in a flash. I only realised this years later.

Different Kinds of Business Sales

Our family didn't speak for almost three months.

What made my dad's trauma worse was that the managers were all complaining. They were scared of computers. They could not see how this could possibly work.

'Your son is out of control,' my father's closest confidants said to him.

The darkness deepened in the family and among the staff. In the ninth month of my being in the business, I presented my dad with evidence of the wholesale theft that his sales manager of 19 years was involved in. The data didn't lie. He addressed it with his sales manager who, after an hour of denial, confessed that he had a massive gambling debt and owed some pretty nasty people money. He had also been drinking to cope with the stress.

A while later, I discovered that Dad's bookkeeper of 14 years was involved in fraud. She was repeatedly issuing credit notes to her mother-in-law's retail shop for stock shipped but never paid for. My dad called her into a meeting and presented her with the evidence. She confided in my father that her 12-year-old son had leukaemia and that they needed the money for treatments.

These two incidents broke my father. We were a year into the turnaround. The banks had regained confidence in us and I had replaced the sales manager and bookkeeper with new talent. The business almost made a profit in that year but my father's mood was darker than ever. I encouraged my parents to take many holidays, and I used the time while they were away to make changes to the business.

Then, we had a major breakthrough when I secured the rights to distribute some of the biggest brands of fishing lures from the

USA. I hopped on a plane to Atlanta, hoping to get a meeting with Lanny West, 30 years my senior and head of marketing at PRADCO – based in Birmingham, Alabama – which stocked America's largest collection of fishing lures. At the time, there were around 39 million registered freshwater anglers in the USA. Established in 1894, PRADCO had recently been purchased by EBSCO, a Birmingham company founded in 1943. Heritage was written all over the company and their leaders and staff were very proud of it. And a little bit arrogant, I thought, having not managed to secure a meeting with them. At the time, there were around 900 000 registered freshwater anglers in South Africa; surely they wanted this business? I knew very little about fishing and although I did fish for recreational purposes every now and then, my true interest and hobby was fast becoming business itself. The audacity of securing the rights for this brand in Africa took great chutzpah, especially given the fact that I had no confirmed meeting with Lanny before leaving South Africa and had only had a few phone calls that I had considered to be positive.

I arrived in Atlanta and hired a car for the two-and-a-half-hour drive west to Birmingham. It took three hours of waiting at reception before Lanny granted me a meeting. He was a lovely, congenial man. He was gobsmacked and inspired by my story and presence. We struck a deal and I won the rights for Africa.

When I arrived home, I went to visit my father. We sat at the same table where, as a four-year-old boy, I used to compile the fishing-lure catalogues.

'Dad, I'm going to market the lures differently this time,' I said.

Lanny had granted us the rights subject to achieving certain sales volumes and I needed to get on with the job.

'What do you mean? Let's do it the way we always have. They have provided you with great full-colour shiny catalogues. Give them to the reps and they can visit clients and take orders. If you have enough of them, we can post them to customers with an order form,' he said with a degree of finality.

'Nope, I'm going to arrange events at our clients' homes. I want them to invite their customers to braais before rugby matches. While they braai I'll demonstrate how the lures swim in their swimming pools,' I replied firmly.

'Don't be ridiculous,' Dad responded. 'It'll take forever, and in any event,' he leaned back, about to deliver his coup de grâce, 'a picture is worth a thousand words.'

I leaned back in settlement and somehow, seemingly out of nowhere, found the right words to counter, 'If a picture is worth a thousand words, an experience is worth a thousand pictures.'

'Dad, check out the numbers,' I said, proudly presenting him the figures one Sunday morning at home.

He faked a smile and said, 'Sure.' He looked at them and nodded. Still staring at the numbers, he asked me what I wanted from the business.

'Dad, more importantly, what do *you* want from the business?' I replied.

Tears welled in his eyes. 'I can't take the stress any longer, and I'm torn. You are doing so well in the business and I feel guilty for having brought you into it. I have no more energy to give to the business. It's been more than 40 years now and I am scared that if the business fails, Mom and I are doomed. We have no money to retire with. And I feel terrible about even sharing this with you. I really want you to carve your own path in life and not be tied through duty or responsibility to the business or me. My biggest regret will be to ever have hindered you or your brother from your true course, whatever it may be.'

Wow. What a father. What a remarkable man. My heart ached seeing him in tears.

'Do you want to sell the business, Dad? Will that take the pressure off, knowing that there will be no risk to you or Mom after the sale?' I asked.

'Only if you want to sell it. I have already taken up prime economic years of your life and am worried that if we sell, you'll be resentful.'

As I said, what a man.

'Let's do it,' I said.

His peace of mind was more important than my ambitions in the business. I loved it and I loved even more what the business was becoming. Truth be told, I already had a 10-year vision for the business in place, something I was unable to discuss with Dad because of the stress he was going through. It was a desperately lonely time for me.

Building the business for sale took some time. My 20s saw me at work from 5am until 9pm every weekday and committing a good 10 hours over every weekend. Four years later, I managed to secure an eight-figure clean sale. It was a beautiful business and had grown incredibly. It remains one of the most valuable experiences I have had in my relationship with my father. The father-son relationship became one of friendship. I do miss him.

Different Kinds of Business Sales

We then have a muddy mix of 'sale closures'. I call them this because they are mostly closures disguised as sales. There are two variations of this.

Disposal

In a disposal, the owner sells the business to a buyer who is often poorly funded for a price that is a fraction of what the seller thought or hoped he or she could get for the business. It almost always comes down to an asset sale in which the assets are sold at auction prices. There may be, depending on the negotiating skills of the parties, a small premium offered for 'goodwill'. Payment stretches over the period of one to three years and is seldom honoured, because mostly these businesses fail to meet the expectations of the parties post-sale. This is the most common type of sale closure, accounting for most of the closure work that business brokers do.

Succession exit

Succession exits are commonplace in family and private businesses. In family businesses, a succession exit can occur for two reasons. Either the founder has been unable to sell the business for an amount that he or she can retire on, or the founder brings his or her children into the business as an opportunity to make something of their future. A succession exit can also take place with management or long-serving employees who want a chance at building the business. In most instances, both the founder and successor have few options. The owner sells the business because he or she needs the money. What makes a succession exit different to a family sale or an MBO is that the seller often has to tolerate long, nerve-wracking terms to allow the business to pay for the sale under the buyer's control.

All of the different kinds of business sales discussed here – outright sales, common sales, MBOs, family sales, disposals and succession exits – account for the 5.4% of all businesses started that ever get sold. The remaining 94.6% of businesses end in closure.

Closure

A simple closure sees you wind down the business, stop trading, let your staff go, dispose of the assets you have at auction prices, give away what you can't sell and hand the keys of your premises back to your landlord. You also have to pay the taxman. It's not a cheap process, so be warned. You then step back, convince yourself that you gave it your best shot and that you did well for yourself and your staff given your circumstances. I saw this happen in my family. My uncle's self-worth collapsed leading up to the closure of his business and accelerated directly thereafter. My family members' anxiety increased exponentially and they aged faster. Imagine your legacy, which took you 40 years or more to build, reduced to vapour!

This future is entirely avoidable. Building a business for sale is not common practice. It has nothing to do with intelligence,

Different Kinds of Business Sales

passion, commitment or hard work. It has everything to do with purpose and know-how. We never start businesses to sell them. Mostly we start them driven by opportunity or necessity. The idea of selling our businesses only becomes apparent much later in our journeys. And then we do it wrong because we lack experience in selling businesses. Most of us will only ever sell a business once or twice, not recognising that the way we build businesses and the way they ought to be built for sale are fundamentally different. This is a problem that we are going to solve today using the knowledge you have gained from this book of what an Asset of Value is and how to build one.

- ❏ There are four types of business sales:
  - An **outright sale**, in which you sell your business for a good price on fair terms and conditions. You are paid in cash, not shares, up front and not over extended periods subject to the business achieving certain targets. There is only a short handover period.
  - A **common sale**, in which you are forced to sell for a low price, paid mainly in shares and not in cash, burdened with demanding terms, conditions and penalties and required to be involved in a long handover period.
  - A **Management Buy-Out**, in which you sell the business to a business successor, typically the current management in the business, for a fair deal.
  - A **family sale**, which is similar to an MBO but involves family members.

- Then there are closures disguised as sales, which we call 'sale closures':
  - A **disposal**, in which the business is sold cheaply, mostly simply as payment for the business's assets, which are sold at auction prices. Payments are seldom honoured.
  - A **succession exit**, in which an owner sells the business to family or long-serving employees with undesirable results for both the seller and the buyer.
- Finally, there is a **closure**, in which you stop operating, let your staff go, dispose of your business's assets at auction prices and pay taxes.
- Forced to close shop, you see your legacy reduced to nothing after many years of sacrifice, investment and effort.
- Most businesses, regardless of their size and age, can still be fixed. It is not too late to act: use the knowledge you have gained from this book to help you achieve the type of sale you and your business deserve.

Conclusion

You are in Control

'I find the greatest thing in this world is not so much in where we stand as in what direction we are moving.'
– Oliver Wendell Holmes Sr

Passion is vital. It's the fuel that feeds your engine. It generates the big vision that in turn gives you meaning in your work and life. It helps you withstand the rough seas, sudden storms and unpredictable currents. Without it, the persistence it takes to build a great business is almost impossible.

If your passion is not entwined with your purpose as a business owner, you risk it turning on you. Passion requires a great deal of idealism, the idea that you, in doing what you do, can and will make the world a better place. Be it in a hotel guest's delight while enjoying a croissant in the morning, the smooth flow of waste water removed from a three-kilometre-deep mine shaft or the gentle squeeze of a lover's hand while a couple gazes at a jewellery-shop window.

And it's okay to obsess over and be single-minded about it. Failing to manifest a business that delivers this idealism to the world seeds cynicism, blame and resentment. Regret about what you should've, would've or could've done differently has little value when time has run out. Fed by your passion, your purpose must be to build your business into an Asset of Value.

Your business is the real product. The goods and services you offer are simply elements of this product. Building your business into a product is the ultimate creative act that sees you transferring your ideas, soul, spirit and talent into something outside of you. It's that act that allows it to live beyond your life, creating your legacy. It's also that act that will see your creative effort and remarkable sacrifices rewarded through a successful sale and exit. It will place you in the 5.4% of all businesses started that do get sold.

There are very few absolute truths in the world. Truth: you are born and, I'm sorry, but you will die. Truth: you cannot change another person; only they can change themselves. Truth: we live in a world of great uncertainty. You can only hope that you will be around tomorrow and you do your best to take care of yourself, but it's not guaranteed. Truth: there is only one thing that you have 100% control over and that is your attitude. Your attitude leads to your behaviour and your behaviour delivers the result in your life. Failed business is as much the harvest of a wrong attitude leading to wrong action as much as it is the harvest of inaction altogether. Pause for a minute from your very busy, noisy day and think carefully about what attitude you hold towards your business. It's an active process of engaging your brain and being honest with

Conclusion

yourself, one that's hard to do alone.

Having read this book and gained an insight into what you need to do to build an Asset of Value, check that your attitude and behaviour are synchronised to ensure that the business you are building will be the product of both your creative act and your sacrifices and that it will give you the return you deserve. Remember, time is the most valuable thing that you spend; it runs out and you can never get it back.

With the courage it took to start your business, the creativity needed to do it differently and the care necessary to sustain it thus far, you have the full set of ingredients that every one of the business owners in this book has. But while increasing your access to knowledge removes ignorance, the real value of insight and foresight is only ever found in action. Through this book and the stories of Clive, Jack and Themba and the many others who I have worked with and continue to work with, I hope that I have managed to share both the mindset and actions it takes to build your business into an Asset of Value.

Notes

1 US Census Bureau (2015). 'Annual Survey of Entrepreneurs (ASE)'. www.census.gov (accessed 12 August 2019).

2 Small Enterprise Development Agency (SEDA) of the South African Department of Trade and Industry (2018). 'SMME Quarterly Update 3rd Quarter 2018'. www.seda.org.za/Publications/Publications/SMME%20Quarterly,%202018-Q3.pdf (accessed 12 August 2019).

3 *Harvard Business Review* (1 January 2012). 'January–February 2012: The Value of Happiness – How Employee Well-Being Drives Profits'. https://hbr.org/archive-toc/BR1201 (accessed 12 August 2019).

www.ingramcontent.com/pod-product-compliance
Lightning Source LLC
Chambersburg PA
CBHW031613210526
45464CB00004B/1555